PSYCHO -LOGIC

How to Take
Charge
of Your Life

A guide to inner success and satisfaction

Bruce D. Hutchison, Ph.D.

Prentice-Hall, Inc.   Englewood Cliffs, New Jersey

Prentice-Hall International, Inc., *London*
Prentice-Hall of Australia, Pty. Ltd., *Sydney*
Prentice-Hall Canada, Inc., *Toronto*
Prentice-Hall of India Private Ltd., *New Delhi*
Prentice-Hall of Japan, Inc., *Tokyo*
Prentice-Hall of Southeast Asia Pte. Ltd., *Singapore*
Whitehall Books, Ltd., *Wellington, New Zealand*
Editora Prentice-Hall do Brasil Ltda., *Rio de Janeiro*

Quotations from "Backstage Behaviorism," by Michael Schulman (p. 116) and "Body Thinking: Psychology for Olympic Champs," by Richard Suinn (p. 150) are reprinted from *Psychology Today Magazine*. Copyright © ·· Ziff-Davis Publishing Company.

Library of Congress Cataloging in Publication Data

Hutchison, Bruce D.
  Psycho-logic.

  Includes index.
  1. Self-perception.   2. Success.   I. Title.
II. Title: Psychologic.
BF697.H8   1983   158´.1   83-3307
ISBN 0-13-732602-5
ISBN 0-13-732610-6 (pbk.)

Printed in the United States of America

Prologue

Most people accept too much about themselves and question too little. It's hard to start finding the right answers until you start asking the right questions. And even then, there are no *final* answers—only answers for now.

Life is always *now.* Even lessons from yesterday and plans for tomorrow are played out in *now* experience. When you open yourself to that experience there is always something in which you involve yourself—to grow on—to move toward. You open yourself to the continuous adventure of discovering who you are and who you still can be.

Bruce D. Hutchison, Ph.D.

Introduction

Psychotherapy is not just an adventure in self-discovery—it's a journey toward satisfaction. Most clients come to therapy genuinely wanting to feel better about themselves. They want to be happier—to get more satisfaction out of life—but are full of excuses about why they can't ...

- I don't even know what real satisfaction is. I've got enough trouble just trying to survive.
- Are you kidding? Satisfaction is for Buddhist monks—and even they have trouble recruiting these days.
- I had a lousy childhood. I blame that on my mother.
- My bad back (education, masochistic lover, spare-tire belly, etc.) keeps me from being happy with myself.

During my early years as a clinical psychologist, I spent a lot of time trying to apply everyone else's theory of psychological happiness, but all the while I kept listening to my clients until gradually I began to decipher the "sense" in what they were saying. No matter how crazy their story seemed when they first started telling it, there was always an internal logic to it when I understood where it came from and how it developed. I began using the term "Psycho-Logic" to describe this unique emotional logic and to emphasize the fact that it was "logical" only within the context of someone's individual life experience. It often made no sense at all by the usual standards of objective logic.

When I stopped applying theories and started listening for this Psycho-Logic, I was amazed at how easy it was to find, and how little my clients were aware of it. Yet when I told them the Psycho-Logic I was hearing, there was often an immediate—and sometimes startling—sense of recognition. Suddenly they could clearly see why their life was working—and why it wasn't.

I quickly learned that Psycho-Logic applied not only to my clients, but to my friends, myself, the groups of businessmen and teachers I worked with—to everyone. I began looking for a method that would allow someone to uncover that Psycho-Logic and to see exactly how it affected his or her behavior, feelings, and the direction of his or her life. At the same time I began searching for a technique—which I later called *Counter* Logic—that would give people the tools to precision tune or rebuild those parts of their Psycho-Logic that they wanted to change.

This book represents the result of my effort and the experience of my clients. Chapter 1 shows you how even small changes in your Psycho-Logic can create a positive impact in the quality of your experience. Chapter 2 is a treasury of new perspectives from which you are invited to choose. The next few chapters describe exactly what Psycho-Logic is, where it comes from, and how and why it develops. Beginning with Chapter 12, you are guided through specific methods for "taking charge of your life"—that is, for modifying those parts of your Psycho-Logic you would like to change. The final chapters show you how to use Psycho-Logic to deal with guilt, depression, and anxiety, and how to enhance the quality of your relationships and sex life.

Acknowledgments

I want to thank my parents, Homer and Georgia Hutchison, for providing all those dinners so I could practice my profession, and for working so I could go to college. Thanks to Donald Pumroy and Donald Nachand for teaching me how to be a psychologist. Special thanks to Carolyn Long for early discussions that helped me formulate my ideas, and for her initial editorial efforts. Thanks to the Psychology Department at the Eastern Shore Hospital Center for feedback when I needed it—Don Nachand, Gordon and Pam Jennings, Bill O'Donnell and Mark Pantle. Thanks to Dusti Jones and Bonnie Michaelson for their professional and personal support. Thanks to Henry for our twenty-year discussion of life I hope never ends. Thanks to Susan for putting up with me while I wrote. Thanks to Melanie for being a beautiful part of my life. Thanks to Sharon Mullinix and Linda Bradford for patiently and accurately typing various versions of this book. Extraspecial thanks to my patients for putting their faith in me.

Contents

1

Making Life Better
from the Inside Out

Where do you stand on a ten point scale of liking yourself? An average "5"? An O.K. "7"? A mediocre "4½"? Have you given up on feeling better about yourself—lost a sense that you could wring more joy and satisfaction out of life?

Life isn't handed to you on a silver platter. There's no how-to-do-it instruction book tied around your neck when you are born. You fumble around and do the best you can. After years of trying you conclude *that is the best you can.* But what if it isn't? What if you just never stumbled across a better way for you? What if a greater sense of success and satisfaction is still within you—like buried treasure hidden in your own back yard? What if all you needed to find it was an idea of where to look and the right tools to help you dig?

There are two methods that can help you find what you're looking for. *Psycho-Logic* is a personal treasure map that leads you to discover the best in yourself. It teaches you what to look for and where to dig. *Counter Logic* provides the tools to do your best with what you find.

Keys to the Treasure

There is more that keeps you from being your best than you realize. Beneath the level of your ordinary awareness is a pervasive emotional logic that constantly influences what you do, why you do it, and how well you carry it out. It affects how your marriage works, how you raise your children, what you expect from relationships, how you get along with your boss, how much income you settle for, your habitual state of tension, your physical well-being, your sexual

17

satisfaction, what you're searching for in life, how much fun you have, and how satisfied you are with yourself. In other words, it affects everything.

This underlying *emotional logic,* and the effect it has on you, is your *Psycho*-Logic. Psycho-Logic is the way you internally organize the important emotional lessons you have learned in your life and how you act on them every day. Psycho-Logic is never truly logical, but it always makes perfect emotional sense once you understand how your inner life operates, and how it came to operate in that particular way.

Psycho-Logic is rarely stated in words, even to yourself. It is such an automatic and natural part of the way you feel and behave, that you simply live by it. Sometimes it sets you up to succeed and feel good about yourself, and other times it keeps you revolving in losing patterns of which you are only vaguely aware.

Counter Logic

Counter Logic is an intentional method for taking charge of your life. It is a way of changing losing patterns, or adding more satisfaction to patterns that are already okay but that could be better. *Psycho*-Logic is automatic. *Counter* Logic is deliberate. Psycho-Logic is based on emotional conclusions reached from life-long experience. Counter Logic is based on *decisions made right now* about the emotional direction in which you'd like your life to move. Psycho-Logic is something to figure out. Counter Logic is what you can do about it.

This book will give a precise method for figuring out your Psycho-Logic, along with Counter Logic techniques for changing those parts of it you would like to change. It's a process that hundreds of my clients have now successfully undertaken.

Robert Kennedy to the Rescue

Janet was a client who started out telling me there was nothing really "wrong" with her life. It just wasn't working. She was single, but that didn't bother her. There was plenty of time left for marriage if she decided she wanted it. She was dating a government bureaucrat with a three-year-old daughter and loved them both—even though she was sometimes tempted to date other men. She had a degree in retailing and had landed a job as an assistant buyer for a well-known chain of clothing stores—lots of trips to New York's garment district and a twenty-five percent discount on all the clothes she bought. Her boss liked her taste and her attention to detail and was already talking about promotion. So why wasn't she happy? Everything seemed to be going her way.

When Janet examined her Psycho-Logic, she realized how important independence was for her. It went back a lot further than women's lib, although liberation did suit her taste. She remembered her father once telling her—she must have been six or seven at the time—"You're gonna be a woman and I'm damn proud of it! Don't let them knock you down, even when you have to stand alone." Janet came home from school one afternoon with a sore elbow and a story about how one of the "rough boys" hit her. "What did you do about it?" her father asked. "I hit him back." "Good!" her father told her, "but don't forget, you're gonna have to outsmart them too."

Janet grew up to be good at taking care of herself—at fighting back and outsmarting her competition—and she liked the feeling of winning that came with it, but her competitive edge was sometimes a little too sharp—especially with men. She often found herself in a battle of wits when she was supposed to be enjoying her dinner. Even when she won, she felt as though she had lost something.

"Sometimes standing up for myself gets really tiring," she said as she thought about it. "I can't seem to get the load off my back. I'll bet I would float right off the ground if I didn't have that load to carry around."

I asked her to close her eyes for a minute and see what image came to her when she thought about being free of that load—of setting it down and just letting herself "float away." The first thing she thought of was hang gliding gently in the sky over a deserted ocean beach—free to climb, or to land, or just float forever. Then she thought of a picture she once saw in *Time* magazine—a picture of Robert Kennedy jogging along an Oregon beach, splashing through the edge of the surf with his pants rolled up to his knees. She told me she had always admired Robert Kennedy's weekend mountain adventures and his whitewater trips down the Columbia River. He seemed to exercise his mentality in work-week Washington and his muscles and spirit in the weekend American wilderness. He seemed to have a way of doing it all. Maybe it was time for her to get in touch with the movement of nature and the rhythm of her own body—to balance things out a little bit better. When I asked her what image might help her keep this idea in mind, she told me, "Robert Kennedy running along that beach." That seemed like good Counter Logic, so we decided to try it.

I told her to take a 3 × 5 file card and write the *Psycho*-Logic she wanted to change, or add to, on one side; and her *Counter* Logic on the other. This is what she wrote ...

Side A

Psycho-Logic

It's important to be independent *all the time* (and have little time left for anything else).

Side B

"RFK" Counter Logic

(1) Independence is not enough any more (I'm tired of being one-dimensional).
(2) Physical adventure, and keeping my body in shape, *is another kind of independence.* (I don't have to give up all my independence!)
(3) Getting close to nature is getting close to myself (I *am* a part of nature).
(4) Float and glide and feel free! (RFK running along the beach.)

I told her to carry her card with her to use as a reminder of what she wanted to add to her life. When she noticed the card, she was to focus briefly on her Psycho-Logic and then on *one* of her Counter-Logic points for a few seconds, several times during the day, until each of these notions had a feeling of spontaneity and naturalness—like a Spanish Vocabulary Card that suddenly clicked into place. Then, and only then, was she to think about actually applying her Counter Logic in her life.

This Counter Logic was a small internal step for Janet, but it was a step that showed her she could begin to choose the direction of her life. Once she had her *internal* compass set, it was far easier for her to see what *external* steps led in that direction.

She signed up for Aerobics at the local YMCA and started dancing her blues away on Mondays, Wednesdays and Fridays. By the time the spring snows thawed she was ordering tent pegs from mountaineering catalogues and planning weekend adventures with her boyfriend, but the changes in her life were not limited to leotards and backpacking. Once she experienced the honest independence of choosing for herself, she suddenly saw choices she never noticed before. Her relationships began to change. Instead of playing substitute mother with her boyfriend's daughter, she was using more of her time to be a child herself—playing in the sandbox with her shoes off and cuddling with Raggedy Ann and her favorite little girl on the living room sofa. Instead of playing around on her boyfriend, she started playing with him—turning her bedroom into a playroom and her bed into a chest full of toys.

She felt exhilarated, playful, childlike, very much excited about what life was suddenly doing for her. "It's like being a child again," she said. Then she thought, "No. It's like being the child I never was." Her "RFK" Counter Logic had given her a start—a clue—a step in the right direction. Now she knew what had been missing—playfulness. She knew it when she found it. Only when she experienced it did she know what she had been searching for. She started a new Counter Logic card with just the title *"Playfulness" Counter Logic* written at the top. She wanted to make sure she didn't lose track of her discovery, and she wanted to find other ways to fit it into her life and keep it in her awareness.

When I saw her a couple of years later she was much happier. She had found a lasting way to back off from things and approach them from an angle of her own choosing. She had kicked her life in the tail and gotten it moving in a direction that was working for her. She had changed her Psycho-Logic. She was married and things were working well. She was truly independent because she had reached the point where she could choose when not to be.

Emotional Survival

At the basis of all Psycho-Logic is an assumption about something an individual feels he or she absolutely *must* have or be in order to feel good or worthwhile. This hidden or partially hidden assumption is crucial to the survival of a sense of self-worth. No one is ever satisfied unless his Psycho-Logic assumptions are being fulfilled, or unless there is some hope that they might be fulfilled in the future.

Psycho-Logic assumptions can be built around children, financial success, intelligence, or any one of a hundred other things that we might come to accept as our way to survive as adequate individuals. Janet learned that independence was essential for her emotional survival.

Until you identify your Psycho-Logic—and the assumptions that support it—there is no way of knowing whether it is moving you in a satisfying direction or holding you back. When you know what your Psycho-Logic is, you immediately increase your power of objectivity. You take the first step toward controlling your Psycho-Logic instead of allowing it to control you automatically.

Taking charge of your Psycho-Logic means being able to ...

(a) State your Psycho-Logic in words—at least to yourself.

(b) Understand precisely when, why, and how it affects your life.

(c) Being able to replace or add to it when Counter Logic alternatives work more effectively.

Legal Craftsmanship

As I've worked with clients, I've seen this kind of precision analysis change a life time and again.

A 42-year-old attorney was not preparing his cases as well as he thought he could. His clients seemed satisfied but he wasn't. When he examined his Psycho-Logic (as you will learn to do in later chapters), he discovered that personal pride—the pride of "craftsman-ship"—was an important emotional issue for him. That was a little surprising. He had a lawyer's tendency to believe in the baser human motives more than the positive ones—even in himself.

In searching for Counter Logic to get back on good terms with himself, he settled on his notion of "craftsmanship." Why not? There *was* a craft in honing and forging and developing a case—in selecting the most telling evidence and presenting it in the most elegant and effective manner. If he really could handle himself like a craftsman maybe he *could* walk away from a case with a craftsman's pride. I advised him to try out his "craftsman" Counter Logic on a single case—using whatever methods this approach suggested. He was delighted with the results. His next court presentation was as smooth as the finish on a silversmith's platter—subtly polished in ways only he knew about. He won the case but, more important, he felt like a winner. He had discovered an emotional lead that showed him how to feel better about himself—that changed his way of handling his own case.

The Second Blooming of Amy

Amy was a housewife who wanted help sorting out her life. She told me she had sunk to the level of *National Enquirer* and "General Hospital"—guilty pleasures she couldn't resist. It was a far cry from her high school heyday when she was a B+ student and secretary-treasurer of the student government. But it seemed as if things were all downhill after graduation. She tried to slide through college by skimming over her notes the way she had in high school. It didn't work. Her freshman college grades dropped from Cs and Ds and she gave up college after her first semester. When I first saw her five years later, our meetings were the bright spot in her week. On the rest of the days she kissed her husband goodbye in the mornings and dug into her dishes and cat litter. Her rose garden was her only remaining passion, and in the fall and winter she didn't even have that.

"Is *this* my life?" she asked, not really expecting an answer. She said she felt shriveled up—like one of the roses that had bloomed in the summer and then closed in on itself after the first frost. I wondered if she could ever see herself blooming again—the second blooming of Amy. I asked her to think about what she might do if she ever blossomed again. This "Second Blossom" Counter Logic turned out to be a good way for her to gain a new perspective. It helped her get around her Psycho-Logic contention that her life had peaked at seventeen. It gave her something to work with—a beginning. In three months she was taking a course in horticulture on public TV and thinking about trade school and the possibility of working in a florist shop.

Combining Forces

In their own ways each of these individuals had turned his or her life around. A lawyer was now working at full capacity and taking pride and pleasure in his accomplishments. Janet was discovering the little girl within her that she had never gotten to know. Amy's gradual slide downhill was beginning to reverse. All of these changes came from a willingness to create more personal satisfaction and a knowledge of how to go about doing it.

Psycho-Logic provides a structure for examining your own life from a new perspective. It shows you how your emotional beliefs were created and how you keep them going. Counter Logic is a method to put *you* in charge of *you*. It shows you how to create *new* experiences that teach you new lessons you choose to learn. When you combine these two forces, you put your foot on a throttle that can accelerate your life and your hand on a wheel that can guide it.

Getting It All Together

A person who is in charge of his or her life and satisfaction is someone who ...

- Understands the Psycho-Logic well enough to control it autonomously, instead of allowing it to control him or her automatically.
- Acts (and reacts) freely and spontaneously in new situations where old Psycho-Logic patterns no longer apply.
- Plans for the future and learns from the past, but gets primary satisfaction from the present.
- Deals with guilt, anxiety, and depression in constructive ways that avoid a Psycho-Logic pattern of chronically negative results.
- Selects and develops relationships that promote joy, intimacy, and mutual respect instead of discouragement, jealousy, and distrust.
- Deals directly with negative relationships without getting his or her own Psycho-Logic mixed up in other people's destructiveness.
- Participates in sex as a celebration of the human body and the human connection without fear, inhibition, or Psycho-Logic game playing.
- Is excited about and open to new discoveries, new adventures, new meaning in relationships, and a constantly expanding sense of who he is and what he is able to do with his life.
- Has the skill and creativity to meet new challenges with new and more effective approaches (i.e., with new Counter Logic).

The Little Engine that Could

Psycho-Logic is based on the premise that you create a lot of your feeling about yourself. If you would like to feel better, you can learn how to do it. If you are already feeling pretty good, you can learn to feel even better. Some of your potential for genuine satisfaction has probably been sidetracked in ways that keep your wheels spinning endlessly on the same track or keep you moving in directions in which you don't really want to go. *Psycho*-Logic can help you discover—or rediscover—the most satisfying track for you, and *Counter* Logic can show you how to restoke your engines so you can start going down that track full steam ahead.

2

Developing Counter Logic:
How to Look at Things
from a New Angle

Cary Grant—a longtime friend of Grace Kelly—once said Grace Kelly always carried herself *as if* she were on top of things long before she ever was. In a magazine interview, the thing Grace Kelly remembered most about her father was his motto, "The harder they hit me, the higher I bounce." It was a way of looking at things that helped her through the early days as a Hollywood starlet and through the difficult transition from American movie queen to Princess of Monaco.

These are not the kinds of problems most of us have, and yet we all go through times when we could use a little bouncing back. Most mothers, for example, lose their babies in the uneasy transition of their growing up. This can be a devastating loss for a mother who has too much invested in "Live For Your Children" Psycho-Logic.

"Live for Your Children" Psycho-Logic

"It's important to love and care for someone (in order to feel important and useful). My children used to need my love and caring but now they're gone. I'll just continue the meaningless routine of caring for the *house.*

This mother knows she should be pleased that her children are grown and able to take care of themselves, but all she feels is a sense of emptiness. She goes through the usual motions of cooking and cleaning, but the house seems too quiet and she catches herself planning Thanksgiving reunion in April. She's depressed, and when she examines her Psycho-Logic, it's easy to see why.

This is the sort of situation where Grace Kelly's perspective, "The harder they hit me, the higher I bounce," might be useful—if it touches the emotional heart of what this woman needs to change, and suggests practical methods for helping her do it. Let's say she decides to stick with Grace Kelly and that the consistent application of this Counter Logic encourages her to "bounce back" into caring for her husband, or bounce out of the house into a more caring arena.

"Bounce Back" Counter Logic

Counter Logic	The harder they hit me, the higher I bounce.
Counter Tactics	1. Get off my duff and do something with my life.
	2. Talk to my husband the way I used to. Find out how he feels these days and share my feelings with him.
	3. Join a gourmet cooking club in order to learn *new* ways of giving—and ways to let others give to me.
	4. Do some of those things I always wanted to do but couldn't when I was too busy raising children.

This woman could have chosen a different Counter Logic that might have led to different (but equally effective) Counter Tactics. That doesn't matter as long as (1) the Counter Logic she does select represents a constructive alternative to the Psycho-Logic she is trying to change and (2) her new perspective leads her to generate Counter Tactics that plug into her current life in a satisfying way. When good Counter Logic is selected, Counter Tactics often suggest themselves.

Something Borrowed, Something New

Useful Counter Logic can come from mayonnaise jars, old Beatle albums, Uncle Max's diary, or anywhere else you can find it. Sometimes the Psycho-Logic you are trying to change suggests an obvious Counter Logic alternative. If it doesn't, you can often create one by turning the problem over in your imagination, or you can ask a close friend for some help. Psychotherapy often amounts to this kind of mutual search for a more productive way of dealing with things. That's what led Janet to develop her "Playfulness" Counter Logic.

Probably the best way to generate effective Counter Logic is to *steal it*. After all, there are no patents on good ideas—or good ways of expressing them. You find them all over the place, just for the taking. Where did Amy get her "second blooming" Counter Logic? She pulled it out of her own analogy. Where did the "legal craftsman" Counter Logic come from? I stole it from my own client and then gave it back to him.

I once stole some useful Counter Logic from my College French teacher. She had college students using crayons to color in "language rivers," and mixing all the colors where the rivers joined to give us a "bird's-eye view" of the elements that made up the French language. Each day, after we finished working in our college coloring books, we would shift our attention from the "bird's-eye view" to what she called the "worm's-eye view" by drilling us on two or three very specific vocabulary words or conjugations. This "bird's-eye, worm's-eye" approach stuck with me. It's been useful when I've been required to come up with a broad "bird's-eye view" plan, as well as a "worm's-eye" way to get the nitty-gritty accomplished.

A Counter Logic Shopping List

What follows is a "shopping list" of forty-six Counter Logic perspectives. Each has been useful to me in one way or another—either in my personal life, or in attempting to help others develop Counter Logic alternatives. I still use many of them. Some have given me a needed inner perspective in a difficult time, or provided a creative solution when I wanted to approach a situation from a different angle. All of them have suggested different tactics at different times depending on the situation I was dealing with.

Like any shopping list, this is a personal one. You may find that some of these perspectives suggest Counter Logic that you can use immediately, either in the language given or in a form that better suits your own situation. The significance of others may only be clear after you've figured out your personal *Psycho*-Logic. In any case, I invite you to change, steal, save, or use anything that might help you generate your own Counter Logic alternatives.

The phrase on the left is the actual Counter Logic, while the explanation on the right is the meaning *I* attach to it. As you go through the list, you might check anything that looks potentially useful. If you feel like changing any of the wording or the meaning, go ahead. Since the list is fairly long, you might want to skim through it for anything that immediately sticks out as useful. If other thoughts occur to you, and they are not on the list, write them in. Anything that strikes you as a good way to look at something is what you're after. Later chapters will describe a method for putting these Counter Logic perspectives into practice.

The Shopping List

"Get it going." Counter Logic	For me, this has two implications—first, that I am responsible for creating my own opinions and getting them moving; and second, that life is the *process* of getting things, and not just the *finality* of having gotten them.
"You *never* arrive." Counter Logic*	Life *is* the train trip, with all the happiness, excitement, adventure, disappointment, and sorrow that goes along with the ride. Stops along the way are only temporary breathing spaces. There is no finality about them, and they are soon left behind as you move on toward the next stop and then the next one after that.
It's not supposed to be fair.	So who said life was *supposed* to be fair? It's actually more fair to you than it is to a lot of people. You are probably still in one piece, with both legs attached, you can read, and you've got enough money to buy this book. Show me someone who finds life fair all the time and we'll both excuse that person from the realities of an imperfect world.
This is a preference (*not* a need!)	I can be relatively happy without what I think would make me absolutely (and forever after) happy. I know that a hundred-million dollars does not bring *automatic* happiness to everyone who has it.
Insecure is human.	Things change. People and life are not always predictable. There is always a certain uneasiness in unknown situations. We all feel inadequate when something seems very

---

*Add the words "Counter Logic" after all these Counter Logic perspectives.

important. Giving ourselves permission to feel uncomfortable relieves us from the burden of unrealistic expectations—and, paradoxically, increases our sense of confidence. It's okay to feel a little uncomfortable. Everyone else does.

Get back (to where you once belonged) (Beatles)

Here's Counter Logic you can sing. I use it to get myself back into an awareness of natural things that used to come more easily for me. This same self-instruction might get you back in touch with something you once knew.

Let it be.

With this I associate, "Do what you can, and let the rest of it be." There is plenty that you *can* do, so concentrate on doing that. A second lesson is for me to *allow* things to be different when I can't change them, or don't want to.

A pain in the neck is not polio!

This helps me to recognize that part of my reaction that is out of proportion to the event. It focuses me on my own dramatics. It helps me when I get too upset about too many things that aren't worth the anxiety I put into them.

I am M.E.

My Experience (M.E.) *is* me. I am no more than the accumulation of what I do, think, or feel during the minutes, hours, and days of my life.

What am I proving here?

This is a question I ask myself when I know there is more to what I'm saying to someone than what I'm saying. Usually I find myself trying to justify part of my Psycho-Logic. When I figure out what it is, I can choose to stop justifying it—or I can choose to justify it better.

That was yesterday.

This helps me get out from under childhood Psycho-Logic when the lady sitting across from me is *not* my mother.

The answer's in the end.

A suggestion from George Harrison in his "Extra Texture" album. This is a thought that reminds me that the answer for any individual is in the sum of his life—*and that answer's not in until that life is over.* Life is a process of *creating* an answer, not waiting for one.

So what?

This is a good thought to counter a tendency to "awfulize." Sometimes I wait for a client to get into the middle of his story of misery and catastrophe and then interrupt him with a rude, "So what?" After a while my interruption becomes internalized and the client finds he is asking himself, "So what?" It's a great antidote for taking himself so seriously.

Life *is* a struggle.	There's a certain amount of frustration in everybody's life. As Zorba the Greek says, "Life is tough, but that's the *joy* in it." Complaining about frustration is like complaining about the law of gravity—they're both part of the way the world turns. We even build conflict into our games and TV sets. So, loosen your belt, dig in your heels, pick a challenge, and grab a piece of the action. If you want an idea of how someone else did it, check out Zorba the Greek.
Nothing is *ever* complete.	Only death is final—and even that remains to be seen. Life flows in cycles—just because you're down (or up) one day or one week or even one year doesn't mean things will inevitably remain that way. An argument can be made that we are only finally lost when we choose to give up.
Happiness is relative.	Happiness comes in spurts, but happiness is by no means beyond our influence. We cannot be "all happy all of the time," no matter what we do, but what we do and how we perceive ourselves can make the difference between 20% happy and 80% happy.
The bait is not the bite.	This reminds me that blaming others for setting me off—when I'm the one who takes the hook—is like blaming the fisherman when the fish is too stupid to tell the difference between a worm and a piece of plastic.
Relax!	I have a whole program of deep muscle relaxation that I have associated with the word "relax." By internally repeating the word "relax," I am able to let the tension flow from my body and put myself at ease and in better control. It's a simple but very useful technique to learn.
Give it away!	A lot of us have Tactics about keeping secrets to protect ourselves or give ourselves a competitive edge. This "give-it-away" Counter Logic helps me understand the opposite reality—the more of myself and my knowledge I give away, the more respect and mutual trust I get back—i.e., that giving freely often gets returned.
Go ahead and play *right now.*	This is a way I give myself permission to have fun without feeling guilty or selfish—or feeling I have to *earn* it first. Most of us deny ourselves immediate pleasures because we have too much work to do or are afraid to enjoy ourselves too much. Why not give yourself occasional permission? It's part of enjoying the immediate experience of life.

While you're waiting for more, use what you've got.	You may *never* have what you consider enough, and certainly not all you want. Nevertheless, there's a whole lifetime to be had in developing and using whatever you do have. Whatever you get *later* is what you will have to work with *then*. Now is now.
Life is terminal.	What if you learned you had a progressive illness for which there was no cure—only certain death in a relatively short time? Is there anything special you would want to do? Do it. *Life* is a terminal illness.
It's only temporary!	The only constant is change. Nothing lasts forever.
You have to do *something*!	The problem of life is filling up the time between birth and death. Unless you decide to end life prematurely, or it ends itself, you will have to do *something* between those limited points in time. Why not do something that creates some meaning for you? Sitting around *is* doing something, but not much.
I forgive Me.	For all the misdeeds, harsh words, and mistakes of ignorance and pure arrogance, I forgive myself and set myself free from the burden of life-long guilt for past mistakes. I also free myself to make amends in any way or any time I choose—or *not* to.
Be in them.	The more I am *into* people—the more I listen to the feelings between their words and see the punctuated language their body speaks—the more I feel with them and a part of them, and the less emotional distance and competition there is between us. It helps me if I think, "How would I feel if I said and *believed* the exact words that another person just said?" I am much less defensive when I get *into* the other person in this way.
Even love has limits.	Love will never fully be the way we want it, but can be more than enough to satisfy us when we are able to accept what it does have to offer.
You don't need *this* one.	There is nothing or no one we couldn't live without. You don't *need* most things, you just *want* them.
Shut up and think!	Stop repeating the same Psycho-Logic and *think*. Your brain is more than a memory device. It also has the capacity to reinterpret creatively.

This too will pass.	This old truism can still help us through temporary pain.
Let it go.	When it's gone, it's gone (whatever *it* is), so Let it go. OR You might want it, but you ain't gonna get it, so you might as well forget it. OR Let this one go, and get on with one you can get. OR How important is it *really*? Let it go. I originally thought of this when I heard a story about a man who loved a bird so much that he squeezed it to death trying to keep it from flying away. Better to let it go.
Stop *trying*!	Do it or choose *not* to do it. Stop half-heartedly "trying." Who are you kidding?
100%	Leopold Stokowski, the orchestra conductor, once walked out of an interview with Dan Rather, because Rather admitted he sometimes worked at only 80 percent efficiency. "I don't talk with anyone who doesn't put in 100 percent," the old man stormed. While Stokowski was conducting, he put in 100 percent. So does Jimmy Connors when he delivers his maximum tennis serve. What would happen if you decided to put in 100 percent in some important area of your life? What if you stopped and instructed yourself at some point during the day, "A hundred percent for the next twenty minutes!" Twenty minutes of total effort, during times of your own choosing, could make a tremendous difference in both the input and output of your effort.
Grab life by the tail!	To me, this connotes *doing* instead of just thinking about doing—of being able to look back on life without regretting a lot of missed opportunities. It involves the Tactics of asking for, instead of meekly waiting for, leftovers.
Mistakes = learning.	Mistakes can be viewed as lessons learned. Why build a failure case against yourself just because something didn't work? A child fails a hundred times before he learns to walk and a student a thousand times before she learns to read. Are these failures? Not if self-correction comes from the feedback of such "mistakes."
Use it or lose it.	I stole this one from a research article about keeping fit in old age, but it seemed to have wider implications. It could also apply to communication in marriage, the muscles of youth, relationships, sexual ability, anger, creativity, and lots more.

One _____ at a time.

This is both an old saying and a TV show. The *blank* can be filled in by saying one *day* at a time—or, as they say in Overeaters Anonymous, one *bite* at a time (instead of twenty bites at fifty calories each), one *page* at a time (instead of the impossible task of a whole reading assignment), one tennis *serve* at a time (like Jimmy Connors' 100 percent on *each* serve), or one *anything* at a time. If you piled a lifetime's worth of food in your front yard, you wouldn't be able to get out the door for the garbage. It's a ridiculous way to think about eating, and no way to enjoy a meal. The flavor of life is in the mouthful on your tongue, not in the one that remains on your plate or you haven't even cooked yet. Savor the flavor.

The *un-critical* eye.

What if we set our critical observation aside for a minute and simply experienced a situation or a relationship without trying to judge it? What if we quit trying to figure it out and simply experienced the qualities that make it what it is? What if we simply allowed its reality to stand freely on its own?

Take good care of yourself; you belong to you.

It is just possible that if you treated yourself kindly, with forgiveness and humility, you would *not* melt. There is a certain Psycho-Logic that goes, "If you're too easy on yourself, you'll never get anything accomplished. After all, you know how lazy you are and how you have to be driven by an inner task master in order to get anything done." If that's so, is it worth it? And if it's not so, is there a Counter Logic approach that could remove the slave driver and get things done anyway?

This is *one* way to do it.

This kind of Counter Logic keeps you flexible enough to change your Tactics as the situation changes, or allows you to modify your Evaluation as you get feedback about how things are going. It can also give you inner permission to respect another person's way of doing things differently.

Try for a *little* better.

When we get too caught up in competing against one another, we have a tendency to devalue ourselves or others by critical comparisons. One way to make positive use of our competitiveness is to use our own previous record as a standard to compete against. A *little* better than your past best performance is always a worthy goal. A *lot* better than that doesn't work unless your past effort wasn't your best effort then. Getting better than someone else happens automatically when you keep getting better than yourself. As Johnny Carson said, when asked about the competition of other talk shows, "Instead of competing, I try to concentrate on doing my own best, and making that best better."

You *choose* to do it. This Counter Logic focuses my attention on the fact that no one is ever standing behind me twisting my arm. I may not like some of the things I do, but no one is making me do them—I am choosing to, no matter how much I complain about it. People stay in bad marriages, or bad jobs, because they *choose* to. Nobody *makes* them. We may have our responsibilities, but we choose to carry them out. There are many realities we cannot change, but we choose our approach to them. It is this awareness that we are *always* choosing that tunes us into other choices—or helps us accept and deal with the ones we make.

Who says so? This self-challenge helps me when I become overawed by someone else's conception of right or wrong, or someone else's notion of what I should or should not be doing. Who are *they*? A lot of the time it's only my own inner voice telling me what "they" might think. By understanding this, I can decide how much of my life I want to turn over to what "they" think—or at least what I think they think.

Misery is optional. (and so is depression, guilt, worry, etc.). Of course, it never *seems* optional, but when you say this phrase to yourself, it's surprising how often it rings true—how often you *are* adding more misery or guilt than is necessary.

This is *it*. I'm sorry your grandmother died, that your complexion isn't perfect, and that a friendship isn't turning out the way you had hoped. I'm sorry for all the starving people in East Africa, the struggling Midwest farmers, and the fact that life is too short. You can change some of these things a little, but there's a lot in this world that you cannot personally change. You don't have to like your limitations, but you have to live within their confines. You can look at it from several angles, but reality always remains whatever it is. A good way to waste your reality is to spend too much time wishing it were different.

From Molehills to Mountains

Counter Logic doesn't change the external reality of the situation, but it does change your way of dealing with it. The right Counter Logic can get you through a date with Godzilla or a weekend at home with your mother. More important, the right *Counter* Logic can help you challenge any lifelong *Psycho*-Logic that is holding you back from your full potential or leading you in the opposite direction.

3

Psycho-Logic:
What It Is and
How It Affects You

If you were taking a test to qualify for a training program, how long would it take you to solve the following mathematical problem?

> A worker got a one-day job picking apples. When he was done, he was paid in apples instead of cash. On his way home he had to cross three bridges, each of which demanded a toll of half his apples plus another half an apple. After he crossed the third bridge he had no apples left. How many apples did he start with?

The answer is "zero." He *started* with no apples. He didn't get paid until the *end* of the first day.

This and similar "trick" riddles try to lead you down a well-learned but erroneous path, while the real answer is embedded in some subtle statement to be taken at face value. This tendency to approach intellectual problems in the same way you approached similar ones in the past is called a "learning set." A learning set often leads you to a correct solution, but not always. In some situations, such as in trick riddles, it can lead you astray by confining your response to a narrow, preset range. At other times it keeps you from using a pair of pliers as a makeshift tack hammer or from using a newspaper as a curtain until you've had a chance to get to the store. A learning set often keeps you from discovering an opportunity, or a pot of gold, down an unfamiliar alley that's not part of your normal routine.

Emotional SETS

A *Psycho-Logic SET* is a learned way of responding under a particular set of *emotional* circumstances. As in intellectual learning sets, its effectiveness depends on how well it fits the current situation—*not how well it worked under the conditions in which it was learned.* A Psycho-Logic SET is much more resistant to change than an ordinary learning set. You don't give up an emotional investment as easily as an intellectual one. The greater your Psycho-Logic investment *in being right,* as opposed to finding the right solution, the greater your tendency to keep adding up numbers rather than looking for another approach to solve the riddle.

The Riddle of Life

Everyone has two or three Psycho-Logic SETs that covertly control most reactions and hundreds of major and minor decisions. Each Psycho-Logic SET follows a three-step internal sequence:

Psycho-Logic SET

S. — Survival Assumption.

This is something you determine you must be or have in order to feel good about yourself. For example, it may be emotionally important for you to be beautiful (or intelligent, independent, or whatever) because sister Mary Lou was beautiful, and look at all the attention she got! Everybody has something he feels he needs to have or be in order to feel happy or self-confident.

E. — Evaluation.

This is your judgment about how much of this essential ingredient you have or think you can get. These self-evaluations tend to be made in extremes. You either see yourself as beautiful (intelligent, independent, etc.) or you see yourself as unattractive (stupid, dependent, etc.).

T. — Tactics.

These are your specific methods for obtaining what you don't have, using what you have, or compensating for what you think you'll never get. This is how you play out your Psycho-Logic. If you're beautiful, it's what you do with your beauty. If you're not, it's your feeling that you'll never be happy, or it may be your decision to go to college and to be smart *instead* of being beautiful.

Even though Psycho-Logic constantly affects the way you feel and what you do, you are usually unaware of precisely what your Psycho-Logic is or the tremendous impact it has on you. Like Musak, it becomes such an integral part of your emotional background that you rarely notice it. You may spend years going to college and succeed at being "smart," without knowing why academic success doesn't make you happy—until you realize that your pursuit of intelligence was just a Psycho-Logic substitute for being beautiful.

When You Chase Your Own Tail, You're Always Three Inches from Your Goal

Carol, at thirty-six, finds herself increasingly dissatisfied with her marriage. She keeps saying to her husband, "You've never been satisfied with me. You just won't accept me the way I am." Carol is right. Her husband does keep asking her to "open up more" and "bring more of herself" to their relationship.

Carol's husband is also right. Carol *is* desperately afraid of getting hurt if she reveals too much of herself. Whenever her husband asks Carol how she feels, she responds to his question by complaining that he doesn't understand her. Revealing her innermost feelings violates her Psycho-Logic. Until Carol, with the help of her therapist, figured out her Psycho-Logic, she was not aware of how it kept her from the intimacy she wanted.

Carol's "Intimacy" Psycho-Logic SET

S. — Survival Assumption.

1) It's essential to be loved.
2) Intimacy is the only proof that someone loves you.

E. — Evaluation.

Since I'm not lovable, no one wants to be intimate with me.

T. — Tactics.

I'll protect myself from rejection by not being intimate with anyone.

This circular reasoning is perfectly designed to prove itself. Since she does not expect intimacy from others, she never initiates any herself. Her Psycho-Logic not only perpetuates emotional distance, but reinforces her anger at others for rejecting her.

Carol's Psycho-Logic makes perfect sense within the context of her life, but is far from being objectively logical. There is no inevitable connection between feelings of love and an ability to communicate them. Even if there were, intimate communication is certainly not the *only* way to demonstrate love. Neither do Carol's retaliatory "I won't be intimate with you either" Tactics logically follow from her Survival Assumptions or her Evaluation. It would have been just as "logical" for her to decide that love is an adolescent illusion no longer worth pursuing, or that she should give up her fruitless search for love and devote herself to her career. She did neither of these because her Psycho-Logic SET, once established, was not open to other alternatives. She didn't do what might have worked because she was too busy doing what didn't.

Trying to Find 1968 with a Map of World War I

The Survival Assumption, Evaluation, and Tactics in a Psycho-Logic SET are merely a shorthand way of defining how someone runs his or her emotional life. They do not tell you where the Psycho-Logic came from or why it took a particular form. The Psycho-Logic SETs that control someone's life make sense only in the context of that person's experience. The only way to truly understand an individual's Psycho-Logic is to understand the specific life events and relationships that led to its development.

My best friend during my Navy days in Italy was Raymond. The main things to know about Raymond is that he is brilliant—his 163 I.Q. was the third highest administrative clerk qualifying score the Navy had seen since World War II—and that he is a klutz who has trouble walking, let alone driving on those narrow Italian roads. At one point in his military career, Raymond reenlisted for three more years so he could use the $2,000 re-up bonus to buy a 1968 Fiat 120. The afternoon he picked up the car, he sideswiped a two-and-a-half-ton tank truck coming at him at eighty kilometers an hour. Raymond and his new car rolled over twice and skidded to a stop through a dozen rows of Italian sweet corn. The car was a total loss, and as Raymond had no insurance he sold the remains to a local junk dealer for \$120, hitchhiked back to base, and reported in for the evening meal—\$2,000 short and three additional years long. That was typical Raymond.

Raymond and I eventually did chip in to buy another car—another Fiat, as a matter of fact—but only after we agreed that I would do the driving and he would do the navigating. Gasoline at the time was fourteen cents a gallon (with military coupons), and since the Fiat was getting thirty-two miles a gallon, we figured we could load up the trunk with free C rations (Raymond and the supply officer were drinking buddies), camp out in our sleeping bags and travel through the southern half of Europe for practically nothing. That would have worked fine if it hadn't been for World War I.

In the evenings when we didn't feel like taking the train into Naples and there wasn't much playing at the post movies, Raymond would retire to one of the back offices, close the door, unfold his Rand McNally road map of Europe, and continue his never-ending compulsion to figure out where the Germans went wrong during the First World War. The idea was to devise a new German strategy that might have won the war for them. Of course, since Rand McNally no longer sold a 1914 version of Europe, Raymond was forced to scratch out a few towns, and rearrange some borders with his magic marker. After completing these preliminary alterations, he proceeded to mark in all the German military movements with wide red arrows and battle dates noted in adjacent red parentheses. French movements were marked with yellow—which was a little hard to see—those of the Americans in orange, and those of the Austrians in purple. Raymond's own ideas for strategy were marked in with the same colors, but his proposed new movements were all made with dashes instead of solid lines. Headquarter units were always indicated with colored stars, and unit strength and corp designations were penciled inside little circles at the center of major staging areas. One look at Raymond's map and it was easy to see why the Germans got so confused during that war.

These strategy sessions and magic marker battles continued for two or three hours, several nights a week for most of the winter and spring before Raymond and I started out on our trip around the European continent. Guess which map Raymond decided to use for navigation? Can you imagine being stuck in the Pyrenees Mountains at two a.m. and almost out of gas, not knowing whether you were headed for Andorra or France because General Richelieu's Brigadoons had tried a surprise attack on the western flank of the Spanish 3rd Cavalry?

Survival Training

Raymond is always working on one of his projects. Besides restructuring World War I, Raymond speaks three languages, is well versed in Greek and Roman mythology, and knows enough chemistry to teach an advanced organic course in college—but it's not only Raymond. His whole family operates from the same achievement Psycho-Logic. His older brother, Joe, is an orthopedic surgeon who avidly reads Japanese historical literature. Joe has taught himself to speak reasonably fluent Japanese by listening to Berlitz "Teach Yourself Japanese" tapes while driving from his home to the hospital where he works. Like Raymond, as soon as Joe finishes one of his projects, he always seems to have another waiting for him.

Raymond's younger brother, Peter, is the twenty-six-year-old failure, and for the same reason that Raymond and Joe are successful. In this family you either "achieve" success by doing something exceptional or you are considered a failure. There is no such thing as "average." Raymond and Joe learned to survive by successfully achieving, and little Peter learned to succeed by failing—and he's done it exceptionally well! Any of the relatives can attest to the fact that Peter is the most successful failure anyone in the family can remember, and their memories go back quite a few generations. Peter never seems to be able to maintain a long-term relationship with a girl, he has been successfully thrown out of three colleges, and has been unable to hold a job for more than a couple of months.

What is the Psycho-Logic that loses Raymond and me in the Pryenees, drives Joe through medical school in the top two percent of his class, and sends Peter through life as a family tragedy? All of these brothers operate from the Survival Assumption that the way to make it in life—and the only way—is through extraordinary achievement. Although they are not aware of this basis for evaluating their lives, it nevertheless influences their thoughts, feelings, and behavior. Their specific Psycho-Logic goes something like this: you are accepted and acceptable only while you are learning or achieving; when you are not doing either, you are a failure and should feel guilty.

Little Peter evaluated his chance of succeeding in this achievement-oriented arena and responded to it very differently from his two older brothers. Without giving up the family Survival Assumption or without changing his Evaluation that he could not measure up to the

Assumption, he adopted Psycho-Logic Tactics that drew him more family attention than both of his brothers and simultaneously vented his frustration at the essence of what the family thought was important.

Raymond's "Achievement" Psycho-Logic*

S. — Survival Assumption.

You can feel good about yourself only when you've done something intellectually significant (i.e., the value of *you* is in what you *do*).

E. — Evaluation.

I'm bright. I can meet these requirements for feeling good.

T. — Tactics.

1. Learn several languages.
2. Constantly study difficult subjects.
3. Never be caught without some intellectual project going.
4. Never be caught with your intellectual pants down.
5. thru 10. Additional tactics about whom to marry, what career to pursue, what friends to cultivate, etc., etc.

Peter's "Successful Failure" Psycho-Logic

S. — Survival Assumption.

You can feel good about yourself only when you've done something intellectually significant (the same Assumption as Joe's and Raymond's).

E. — Evaluation.

I'm not smart enough to beat them intellectually, but I can outsmart them by being the "best worst."

T. — Tactics.

1. Fail in school.
2. Fail at work.
3. Fail in relationships.
4. thru 10. Other specific Tactics for failing successfully.

---

* Surgeon brother Joe's Psycho-Logic is similar to Raymond's. Only the Tactics differ.

Raymond and little Peter start out with the same Survival Assumption, but end up with opposite Evaluations and completely different Tactics.

Looking for a Crack Between a Rock and a Hard Place

When any of the three components of a Psycho-Logic SET change, so does the effect that SET has on the life involved. *Because Survival Assumptions have survival importance, they are the least amenable to change.* Survival Assumptions are often seen as basic, unalterable aspects of the personality.

Tactics are the most pliable elements in a Psycho-Logic SET because they can be altered without significantly affecting the emotional direction in which someone is moving. There are many emotional roads to Rome, and many Tactical ways to approach the same Survival Assumption. If marital success is essential for "happiness," it's possible to change partners or marital styles without affecting the "happiness-through-marriage" Survival Assumption.

Evaluations fall between Survival Assumption and Tactics. They are moderately pliable, but tend to change rather slowly—often well after a change in fact. When someone Evaluates himself or herself as overweight or intellectually dull, that Evaluation tends to stick long after the body thins down or the mind sharpens up. This internal time lag accounts for the thin dieter who still "feels fat" or the newly blossomed student who still thinks of himself or herself as "dumb."

The Cola Prostitute

In talking about adolescence with an aging Manhattan prostitute, Studs Terkel quotes her as saying, "I was very lonely. I didn't experience myself as being attractive. I had always felt I was too big, too fat, too awkward, didn't look like a [cola girl] ad, was not anywhere near The American Dream. Guys were mostly scared of me. I didn't know how to play the games right. I understood very clearly that they were not attracted to me for what I was, but as a sexual object. I *was* attractive."

What is this woman saying about her Psycho-Logic? By the time she was a teenager she already felt left out of her own cola girl dream and had Evaluated herself as totally awkward in playing the flirtation game that all the attractive people seemed to play so well, but she was stuck with a Survival Assumption that attractiveness was the crucial winning attribute in her adolescent world. She wanted to be attractive, but saw homeliness reflected in her mirror, and in the eyes of the "beautiful people" she envied. What Tactics could she use to resolve this conflict?

Then comes the cola Psycho-Logic—when you are able to attract you *are* attractive. This Psycho-Logic play on words tells her what to do. The rest of her life is devoted to her personal version of the cola prostitute. She not only has a substitute way of feeling attractive, but also has devised an inner scheme for taking her pent-up resentment out on the men who ignored her. Now she has something *they* want, instead of the other way around.

"I was in control with every one of these relationships. You're vulnerable if you allow yourself to be involved sexually. I wasn't. They were. I called it. Being able to manipulate somebody sexually, I could determine when I wanted that particular transaction to end...I could play all kinds of games. See? It was a tremendous sense of power."

Of course, the TV commercials never show a cola girl growing old, or even hint that the external pursuit of attractiveness can eventually ruin your life.

"You become your job. I became what I did. I became a hustler. I became cold, I became hard, I became turned off, I became numb. Even when I wasn't hustling, I was a hustler. People aren't built to switch on and off like water faucets."

In a few short bits of conversation we began to see the Psycho-Logic that lies behind a life.

"Cola Girl" Psycho-Logic

S. — Survival Assumption.

It is essential to be cola girl beautiful. That's the only way to attract men and get in on all the flirtatious fun and games.

E. — Evaluation.

I'm not cola girl beautiful, but I am attractive as a sexual object.

T. — Tactics.

I'll use sex to attract men (and to put me in charge so I won't get rejected anymore).

This was a "better-than-nothing" Psycho-Logic compromise of a very painful adolescent dilemma. As this young girl's Psycho-Logic

SET crystallized in her life, and she refined her Tactics for playing it out, it *became* her life—and eventually, her personal tragedy.

Beauty as the Beast

Suppose this girl had never developed the Survival Assumption that beauty is essential for survival? The issue would have been resolved before it began. There would have been no need to Evaluate or develop Tactics around something that was not emotionally relevant.

Suppose the Psycho-Logic had gone this way ...

S. — Survival Assumption.

It's important to be a cola girl. You get the most attention that way.

E. — Evaluation.

I am ugly and unappealing.

T. — Tactics.

If I study hard and get all As, maybe I could get attention for that—even though it's not exactly the kind I want.

Or this way ...

T. — Tactics.

If I get pregnant I might get someone to marry me—or at least have a child who will love me even if I am unattractive.

Or this way ...

T. — Tactics.

Since no one loves an ugly person, I resign myself to a life of misery and loneliness. I will devote myself to hiding away from people.

Suppose the Logic had gone this way ...

S. — Survival Assumption.

It's important to be a cola girl.

E. — Evaluation.

I *am* a cola girl. I'm beautiful.

T. — Tactics.

   I will use my looks to get all I can from people.

At first glance, this last resolution may seem like an ideal situation but, as any cola girl can tell you, beauty brings its own kind of dangers and disappointments. If you learn to rely on it too much, what do you do when it's gone? And even while you've got it, what do you do about the exploiters who shoot down beautiful targets and then turn their attention elsewhere when another potential trophy comes along? Like anything else in life, satisfaction comes from how you use what you have as much as what you have to use.

Whatever Psycho-Logic you develop goes a long way in both defining and confining you. It always involves a certain element of mental prostitution—that is, you are willing to accept and internalize some negative ways of thinking about yourself if that will buy you a secure emotional position. In the end, it's a trade-off. Once you find a Psycho-Logic that tells you what you are, negative or not, you are likely to cling to it with some tenacity. It is not unattractiveness that does you in as much as the meaning you develop around it. Studs Terkel's hooker was a prostitute in her head long before her body turned its first trick.

Which Chicken Did the Egg Lay First?

The specific wording of a Survival Assumption is always derived from the particular element on which the individual is emotionally focused. For one person, it may seem essential to have that special kind of attention you get only when you're beautiful. For someone else, it may simply be important to have a great deal of attention, even though beauty happens to be the usual way of attracting it. In the first situation, the *importance of beauty* would be the core of the Survival Assumption while in the second case it would be the *importance of attention*. The Tactics, however, could easily be the same for both individuals if both were beautiful and both used their beauty in the same way.*

---

   * Theoretically, the more narrowly restricted "importance of beauty" Survival Assumption would leave fewer Tactics available for its fulfillment.

What Is Psycho-Logic?

Your Psycho-Logic consists of those two or three Psycho-Logic SETS that control most of your emotional life. It's something all people have, whether they know about it or not. Like breathing, it works beneath the surface, where it takes care of your survival without your being much aware of it.

Psycho-Logic is the cumulative product of your experience and the conclusions you draw from it. Its purpose is to make emotional sense out of a complicated and often contradictory world, and to give your emotions stability and direction.

The Good and Bad of Psycho-Logic

Is Psycho-Logic positive or negative? Is it OK or self-destructive? Psycho-Logic is neither. It's amoral. It's simply a description of *how* you operate. The *effects* of Psycho-Logic, however, can be either constructive and uplifting or tragic and self-defeating. Psycho-Logic is like a hammer that can either build *or* destroy. It's up to you to decide which parts of your Psycho-Logic are helping you in a positive way and which are negative and self-defeating. In upcoming chapters you will be learning methods for uncovering your Psycho-Logic and specific techniques for making changes, but *which* changes you make will depend on your own priorities and values.

4

Oldies but Goodies,
Psycho-Logic Themes,
Part I

Psycho-Logic Survival Assumptions come from basic needs that have at least some importance for all of us. We all need to be loved, or at least recognized or paid attention to, and we all need to have a sense that we are worthwhile in some way—at least to ourselves. These kinds of basic needs fall into eight general categories: physical survival, love, approval, stimulation, structure, self-reliance, power, and accomplishment. This chapter deals with the first four of these basic needs, along with common Psycho-Logic themes associated with each of them, while the next chapter considers the remaining four needs and their related Psycho-Logic themes.

The "Basic Eight"

The way in which each of these eight basic needs is met at certain crucial stages of life determines its ultimate Psycho-Logic importance. As many of the examples in Chapter 4 suggest, needs that are overmet (such as too much love or too much structure) or undermet (not enough love or very little structure) are particularly conducive to the development of a self-defeating Psycho-Logic. These eight basic needs, in one guise or the other, are at the root of most Survival Assumptions. The particular form a Survival Assumption takes, however, can vary considerably, even though there is a tendency for Survival Assumptions to cluster around certain common themes.

The theme variations considered here are those most frequently seen in each need category. These themes are given colloquial names, such as "Lone Ranger Logic," "Permission to Go to the Bathroom," and "Flirt," because this seems to be the most descriptive way of referring to them.

1—Physical Survival

Obviously no other need has any importance unless the need for physical survival is met. We take for granted that we will always have the nurturance, oxygen, and biological support systems necessary for physical survival, but no one takes breathing for granted while he's drowning. When one of these support systems is suddenly interrupted, total attention instinctively narrows to the immediate matter of life or death.

Most of the time physical needs do not play a significant part in the development of Psycho-Logic since they are usually met at some minimal level, and always have been. There are, however, exceptions. A college professor I know has a reputation for throwing huge parties in his kitchen—which by no coincidence is the largest room in a house he designed himself. He was raised in an orphanage where he was rarely allowed to eat between meals and never allowed to raid the refrigerator. Now he's forty-five pounds overweight and one of his favorite treats is going to the refrigerator anytime he feels like it. Even though his Psycho-Logic is not literally based on physical survival, it does center around a primary survival need.

"Refrigerator" Psycho-Logic

S. — Survival Assumption.

It's important to eat whenever I want to (to satisfy my hunger for food *and* my hunger for a sense of freedom and control over my life).

E. — Evaluation.

What I couldn't do as a child, I'll damn well do as an adult.

T. — Tactics.

1. Build a huge kitchen.
2. Throw parties in my kitchen.
3. Go to the refrigerator whenever I want to.
4. Gain an extra forty-five pounds.

As most dieters know, there is a great deal of Psycho-Logic around eating that is not related to physical hunger. If people ate only when they were hungry, very few would be overweight.

Psycho-Logical Thin Air

Psycho-Logic can be built around any primary need. I once treated a phobic client who experienced suffocation panic every time she felt trapped in a crowd. She would frantically choke and gasp for air until she was able to escape the feeling of terror that came from imagining all those people closing in around her.

She was born on December 23, 1955—four months after her mother's forty-second birthday and just a year before her only brother graduated from high school. She had always felt uneasy around her brother and even more uncomfortable around the children her own age. She never had a close girlfriend and didn't start dating until she was nearly seventeen. By that time her adolescent fantasies were filled with heros from Gothic movies and a strong, quiet man to rescue her from the lonely tedium of her high school reality. She fell instantly in love with the first boy who took her to bed and settled into two years of matrimonial daydreams—until all her dreams suddenly died on a Sunday afternoon in May when the only boyfriend she had ever known announced his enlistment in the Air Force. On the day he left for Texas the idea of suicide flashed through her mind for the first time, but the thought was so frightening she refused to dwell on it. Instead of dying, she simply gave up living.

For the rest of that long, empty summer it seemed as though everyone knew how totally rejected she felt. People seemed to stare at her much too long, or look away too quickly when they saw her coming. She started hiding in her bedroom, staring at the ceiling for hours, while her father peered over his glasses every time she came downstairs and her mother tried to get her to take multivitamins and eat more of what was on her plate. In the fall of that year she managed to get a job as a teacher's aide at a neighborhood elementary school, but felt so uneasy with the children that she was finally dismissed for coming late once too often. She began spending more time alone in her room, and feeling more anxious whenever she left it—especially when people were around. She refused to go places. After several months, she was able to enter a supermarket late at night only when she was sure it would be empty.

When her father found out about this latest supermarket phobia, he decided it was time to put an end to her imaginary fears once and for all. He forced her in the car and drove her to the Safeway on a crowded Saturday morning, led her by the arm to the back of the store and left her standing there while he waited out front.

As she watched him hurrying away, she could feel her hands starting to tremble and the room starting to turn. She began running down one of the aisles but banged into something. Cans started falling and rolling across the floor. Everyone was staring at her. The noise of the cans and the people and the carts banging split right through the middle of her head. She knew everyone could see through her mind—right into her secret thoughts and fears. There was no escape. She was hyperventilating—suffocating. She thought she was dying. What a relief it would be! But she didn't die.

After that horrible day she stopped going to the movies and restaurants, then wouldn't leave the house at all. She couldn't escape the feeling that she would suffocate if she went out. When her parents finally sought professional help, treatment had to begin in her bedroom. It took several weeks of therapy before she was able to leave that room, and several months before she began to understand her Psycho-Logic fear, but she was eventually able to recognize and deal with it in a way that no longer terrified her.

Her "suffocation" Psycho-Logic went like this:

S. — Survival Assumption.

It's essential to breathe (i.e., live), even when part of me wants to commit suicide.

E. — Evaluation.

I can't breathe (i.e., live) with large crowds of people staring at me—reminding me of all my secret feelings of rejection, and my secret desire to escape everything.

T. — Tactics.

I can keep myself alive (and from feeling rejected) only by staying out of crowds.

In addition to crowd phobias, there are food phobias, bug phobias, height phobias—and a frightening long list of others that sometimes trap people inside their houses or even in one room or a closet. When actual physical survival is not at stake, these reactions can only be understood in terms of Psycho-Logic that supports them.

2—Need to Be Loved and Cared For

The instinctive need for food, air, and water can easily be understood in biological terms, but how do such intangibles as love or power become needs around which Psycho-Logic can develop? From the moment of birth the physical presence of another human being is a critical link between immediate physical survival and no survival at all. We initially learn to need people because we don't eat, stay comfortably dry, or get touched without them. The inevitable association between survival and human contact teaches a powerful human connection from which we never fully recover. It is this early association that forms the foundation for human love and compassion.

But while we are gradually learning to care for and depend on people, we also learn that they are not always dependable. As we struggle to meet our physical and emerging relationship needs, Psycho-Logic begins to develop around our perception of what we get from other people and how we might go about getting a dependable supply of it. As we grow older and more physically independent, the primary needs for food, shelter and warmth become easier for us to attain on our own, while our growing needs for love and other intangibles become increasingly complex as unpredictable people become increasingly necessary for their fulfillment.

The Art of Raising One's Hand Before One Goes

Permission to Go to the Bathroom (PTGTB) is a Psycho-Logic theme that utilizes overdependence and self-subordination as a means of securing love from people. PTGTB Psycho-Logic says, "If I always do what people want me to do, they'll always love me for it." PTGTBs incessantly ask others what to do, check to see if what they are doing is OK, or simply look for inadvertent clues to help them figure out what others want from them.

These Tactics form a match with someone who operates from power-authority Psycho-Logic. If it feels good to give permission, it's useful to have someone around who asks for it. In most relationships, however, a PTGTB's constant demand for guidance and reassurance is so intense it drives people away.

Peeking Out of the Closet

No one would have suspected that Barbara was a closet *Permission to Go to the Bathroom*. She always seemed so sure of herself. At thirty-three she had her master's degree in Business Administration and had already moved three steps up the managerial ladder of a respected pharmaceutical firm. At weekly staff meetings, Barbara appeared to be outgoing, confident, and—most of all—decisive. She had a knack for getting to the essence of a complicated issue and for backing up her arguments with facts and firmness. She made decisions and stood by them, but still went along with the majority when the vote went against her. In the everyday friction of her intimate relationships, however, Barbara's crystal-cool facade suddenly melted away. Whenever a decision involved a close friend or lover, she simply couldn't make up her mind about anything without compulsively and incessantly asking their advice (i.e., getting them to make the decision for her).

By figuring out her Psycho-Logic, Barbara discovered that she had modeled her external strength on a determined but emotionally distant father, while simultaneously acquiring an internal weakness that came from feeling intimidated in such a relationship.

Barbara's "PTGTB" Psycho-Logic

S. — Survival Assumption.

It's essential to be loved and accepted (by big, strong Daddy).

E. — Evaluation.

I'm not loved or accepted (by Daddy), but if I do whatever a strong person wants (Daddy, lover, husband, boss, etc.), that person might eventually accept me.

T. — Tactics.

1. Seek out strong people and keep asking them what to do (implicitly or explicitly) until I'm sure I know how to please them.
2. Pretend to be externally strong to cover up my internal weakness.

Droopy Eyes and Waggy Tail

A second Psycho-Logic theme on the need to be loved and cared for is *Cute Little Puppy*. This involves "please take care of me" Tactics which take this general form:

"Cute Little Puppy" Psycho-Logic

S. — Survival Assumption.

It's essential to be loved and cared for all the time (by *everyone*, by *one* specific person, or by *any* person).

E. — Evaluation.

I can't care for myself (make decisions, figure out what to do with my life, fix my own dinner, etc.).

T. — Tactics.

I'll act like a "cute little puppy" so someone will pick me up, pat me on the head, and put my food and water out every night (i.e., make my decisions, clean up my mess, let me out for a walk, etc.).

PTGTBs and *Cute Little Puppies* both lack sufficient self-love and self-respect, and rarely get enough from others to fill their endless emotional demands.

3—Need for Attention and Approval

Most people need some approval and attention, at least some of the time. A few manage to get along well with little of it, while others never seem to get enough. Even though attention and approval are not synonymous, they are often functionally related, since approval is itself a powerful form of attention. It's hard to approve of someone without paying attention to him or her. Attention and approval are particularly difficult to separate in an ongoing relationship since many exchanges involve a combination of the two. Nevertheless, one or the other may predominate in any particular Psycho-Logic SET.

In a peculiar sort of way, *dis*approval can also be a powerful form of positive attention. As we saw in the case of Little Peter's "successful failure" Psycho-Logic, what looks like disapproval can sometimes be the exact kind of approval someone is seeking. A frustrated wife or husband who gets little or no attention from a spouse may resort to Tactics that generate disapproval but at least gain attention. Little Peter is far from alone in his discovery that negative attention is sometimes better than no attention at all.

Seals on Your Forehead

There are a number of ways that a basically healthy need for attention and approval can be Psycho-Logically subverted. *Seal of Approval* Psycho-Logic is one. This describes the person who constantly seeks external confirmation that who he is and what he does is worthwhile. He develops subtle and not so subtle ways to openly display his accomplishments—as if to say, "Hey, take a look at what I've done! Is it OK?" Rather than seeking prior approval for what he does (as in *Permission to Go to the Bathroom*) a *Seal of Approval* is able to make initial decisions independently, but can't resist seeking validation after the fact.

Sunshine in the Sunday Room

A psychologist friend of mine, who has spent the last three years writing a book, remembers a telling incident when he was about four. He was visiting his grandparents in the factory town of Glens Falls, New York, about forty miles up the Hudson River from Albany. It was Christmas, and all his aunts, uncles, parents and grandparents— there must have been thirteen or fourteen altogether—were gathered in the Sunday Room, which was used only on Sundays and special occasions. Everyone was in a circle around the room and my friend was on stage in the center of a huge braided rug. It was theater-in-the-round. His Aunt Louise was playing, "You Are My Sunshine" on the Victrola and he was mouthing the words while the others were squirming in their seats, jabbing each other in the side and yelling, "Isn't he the cutest little thing you've ever seen!" When the performance was over, my friend went around the circle and kissed all the aunts, while each of the uncles slipped a nickle or dime in his pocket. As the oldest grandchild, of what later turned out to be twenty-three on one side and seventeen on the other, he was clearly something special. It was a position from which he was still trying to recover— and which he was still trying to recreate—when I met him twenty-five years later.

What Psycho-Logic meaning does this memory have for him? Here's the *Seal of Approval* Psycho-Logic that goes with it:

S. — Survival Assumption.

It's important to be the center of attention and totally approved of.

E. — Evaluation.

That once happened automatically, but somehow got lost as I got older.

T. — Tactics.

Find a way to get it back again.

Obviously this is a less-than-perfect resolution. For one thing, he would *really* like to get back to being the number one attention-getter without having to earn it, although his Psycho-Logic resolution implies some awareness that it isn't going to happen by magic anymore. Much of his adult life has been devoted to missing this magic kingdom. Going to a party full of strangers is sometimes like going to a Sunday Room full of strangers—and having to compete with thirty other grownup kids for *his* attention. Nobody asks him to sing "You Are My Sunshine" and nobody sticks any nickels in his pocket. He has been able to get some party applause by getting good at telling jokes, but that still means working for attention, and somehow it just isn't the same. The attention is supposed to be automatic, free, and inexhaustible.

Seal of Approval is part of the Psycho-Logic that pushed him toward a Ph.D., and it is his primary motivation for writing a book. He tells me, "I can see it all now. There I am signing autographs in the middle of a huge book store in Chicago, just after appearing on the "Donahue" show. Everyone is saying how wonderful the book is and how clever I am for writing it. Suddenly the public address system starts playing, 'You Are My Sunshine.' I jump up on the autograph table and start mouthing the words, while everyone starts jabbing each other with their elbows and saying, 'Isn't he just the cutest little book writer you ever saw!' Wow!"

Don't Misunderstand if I Put My Hand on Your Knee

Flirt is an attention-getting strategy based on sexual bait to hook the desired approval. *Flirts* are easily identified by their couturier appearance and flirtatious nonverbal behavior. They emphasize hair grooming, coordinated designer outfits, hip-hugging jeans, and a general Barbie doll-Ken doll look. Their matching behavioral style includes subtly suggestive body movements and posturing, overly flirtatious greetings, indiscriminate touching, lingering conversations, leaning forward with exaggerated interest, and eye contact that is uncomfortably long. The cola prostitute, in her prime, exemplifies the extreme of these Psycho-Logic Tactics—although they are more often played out less blatantly. Even though they are usually thought of as feminine Tactics, they are actually used as much by men as by women. Many men who can't or don't use them are jealous of those who do.

This *Flirtatious* bid for attention is ordinarily denied by those who use it most openly. They argue that it isn't their fault that they happen to be attractive, or that their latest male or female friend gets jealous so easily. Other people simply misunderstand their friendly gestures.

Send in the Clowns

A third bid for attention/approval involves *Court Jester* Psycho-Logic. (Variations include *Joke of the Day, Life of the Party,* and *Office Claribelle.*)

A *Court Jester* develops a comic routine to gain approval and attention, along with a comic mask to hide behind. By giving a performance instead of himself, he is able to draw laughs and approval without revealing anything personal. A *Court Jester* is often the sad clown with the painted smile, hiding behind his tricks and makeup. His jokes and routines vary as he adds new material, but the constant purpose of his colorful performance is attention-getting camouflage.

One overweight *Court Jester* was being only partly fallacious when he referred to his life as a "big fat joke." When he was a child, his weight earned him the nickname of Fatty Arbuckle—a self image that was still with him, even though no one called him that anymore. He quickly learned to beat his tormentors to the punch line by telling fat jokes on himself. Twenty-seven years later his repertoire had widened, along with his pants size, but his Court Jester routine remained the same.

"Fatty Arbuckle" Psycho-Logic

S. — Survival Assumption.

It's essential to be approved of and accepted (in order to approve of myself).

E. — Evaluation.

I'm disapproved of and rejected because I'm too fat.

T. — Tactics.

Get other people to accept me by joining them in poking fun at me.

One problem with these Tactics is the tendency to get trapped in your own Psycho-Logic. In order to avoid being tormented, you become your own worst tormentor. The loss in self-respect is often greater than the attention gained.

Have You Heard that Millie Got Pregnant by a Wart Toad?

Gossip is a form of Psycho-Logic used to gain attention by being the first on the block—or in the office—with the juiciest rumor or most recent soap-opera tidbid. Like the *Court Jester,* a *Gossip* has a high Psycho-Logic need for attention, but is genuinely uncomfortable revealing personal thoughts or feelings. She talks about the latest divorce or most recent addition to the office hit list as a way of gaining attention without telling you what's going on with her.

All of the Psycho-Logic Tactics that emerge from the need for attention or approval represent an indirect way of asking, "Am I OK?" In mild forms, they do little harm and can be an effective way to meet the basic human need for confirmation. At more severe levels, however, the need for confirmation becomes so intense that no amount of attention or approval can fulfill it.

4—Need for Stimulation

It takes less than half an hour of total isolation to drive most people to the brink of hysteria. Experimental subjects deprived of sensory input from all five senses usually begin to hallucinate in about twenty minutes. After that, paid volunteers refuse to remain in an isolation chamber for an extra twenty dollars a minute!

Even in the comparatively high sensory conditions of ordinary life, people often get bored and look around for something novel to stimulate their senses and start their neurons firing a little faster. Most psychologists believe that the need for sensory stimulation is as basic to life as the need for food or water.

Research has found differences in responsiveness to stimulation that exist from birth and that remain fairly constant, at least through the first few years of life. As children grow toward maturity, however, a stimultaion-excitement form of Psycho-Logic can also develop as an acquired life style. One such stimulation-excitement theme is *James Bond* (or *Jamie Bond*) Psycho-Logic.

007

A *James Bond* seeks stimulation and tackles new challenges with a great deal of energy and enthusiasm. He is a thrill seeker constantly on the prowl for a new adventure, a new job, a new relationship or a new anything. He is as terrific at starting things as he is terrible at following anything through. Most of his initial enthusiasm fades quickly as he leaves the old behind, at least emotionally, and renews his search for something more exciting.

When *James Bond* Psycho-Logic involves relationships, especially romantic ones, there is a tendency to vacillate between keeping an excitement score by body count or, at the opposite extreme, to search for the never-ending excitement of eternal romance. The stimulation of early romantic feelings, which are frequently confused with love, is predictably disappointed when the feelings inevitably lose their sparkle.

James Bond "True Love" Psycho-Logic

S. — Survival Assumption.

Eternal romance (excitement, adrenalin flow, inability to concentrate) is an essential ingredient for a stimulating life.

E. — Evaluation.

Love and romance are the same. If I don't feel romantic, I must not be in love.

T. — Tactics.

Keep changing partners in search of true romance that lasts forever.

Split-Level Runaway

For Lois, there was never much doubt that her primary Survival Assumptions centered around home, comfort, and middle-class stability—or about as far from *James Bond* Psycho-Logic as anyone could get.

Lois had always made better-than-average grades in college but had gotten her liberal arts degree in "practically nothing" because she wasn't interested in anything practical. Job market practicality just wasn't part of her "two kids, husband working, split-level" dream. After nine years of marriage and two children, Lois felt as if she was drowning in car pools, PTAs, weekend-only sex, and dinners every night at 5:15. She was bored. She had been through the usual distractions—Book of the Month, aerobic dancing, totally tennis—but nothing seemed to relieve her growing sense of aimless wandering. The only thing she hadn't tried was working, but with her limited job skills, all she expected from that was more meaningless routine for a little extra spending money. At the end of one especially long summer, she half-heartedly enrolled in a work-study program in Licensed Practical Nursing at a University Hospital. When she first walked down those crowded hospital corridors, her stomach reminded her of other uneasy corridors on other first days, but after a couple of weeks, she was beginning to notice a return of the confidence she used to have in college. She was a quick learner and everyone seemed to be pleased with the way she handled herself. All of a sudden there was a lot of feedback about how competent and attractive she was. She was coming alive again and making new friends, especially two unmarried nurses who liked to stop for a drink after work to get the taste of formaldehyde out of their throats. They called it their "attitude adjustment hour" and it seemed to fit perfectly with Lois's own readjusting attitude.

She started going to concerts and little theatre productions with her friends, leaving her husband behind when he complained that he was too tired to go or too disinterested. Lois knew she was leaving him behind. She was moving forward again while he was standing still. After one bad argument, when she came home an hour and a half later than she was "supposed to," she realized there was very little left between them. She knew she had already divorced him emotionally. It would just be a matter of time before they went through an actual separation.

There was no turning back. Lois wanted a life filled with the challenge and excitement she had finally tasted. She wanted a career of her own and friends of her own. She wanted a new relationship with a new man. She wanted a lover. In fact, she wanted several of them. She had come a long way from her original Survival Assumption based on traditional home and family values. That had never given her what she dreamed it would. Now she wanted to bask in the limelight of independence, instead of hiding in the shadow of marriage.

The gradual or sudden realization that life has not turned out the way it was anticipated can sometimes generate this kind of change in Tactics, or even profoundly alter a lifelong Survival Assumption.

Lois's "New Adventure" Psycho-Logic

S. — Survival Assumption.

Life is boring without a sense of success, challenge, and stimulation.

E. — Evaluation.

Now I realize that excitement is important and that I can have more of it than I settled for.

T. — Tactics.

1. Get a challenging job that gives me a lot of stimulating feedback.
2. Go places by myself or with friends, even when my husband won't go.
3. Involve myself in new and stimulating relationships, activities, etc.

This kind of drastic change could affect one area of life or many areas, since *James Bond* can be played out in single aspects of life, such as the excitement of frequent career or relationship change, or it can be played out in a broader life scale, when any new form of excitement will do.

Dog-Day Afternoon

Another Tactic used to generate excitement in a dull relationship is *"Tease The Sleeping Dog"*. This involves picking a fight for the Psycho-Logic purpose of livening things up. It's classic George and Martha Tactics in *Who's Afraid of Virginia Woolf.* Nothing gets the blood circulating faster than a little controversy, and that extra jolt of adrenalin often livens up the bedroom antics when the shouting match is over. Many couples find they are able to communicate honestly and intimately only after a battle. By relieving some of the tension and venting built-up hostilities, they momentarily free themselves to communicate authentically.

5

Psycho-Logic Themes, Part II

Round and round and round you go and where you stop you'll never know. Psycho-Logic themes repeat themselves like a needle stuck in the groove of an old record. Click, click, click. The same theme keeps running through your head until you know it without hearing it—hear it without knowing it. If the Psycho-Logic theme fits harmoniously, it adds sparkle and confidence. If the theme has too many sour notes—if it doesn't fit with the times or leads you to dance a jig while everyone else is waltzing—you become out of sync with yourself and with everyone around you.

This chapter examines how people get stuck in Psycho-Logic themes related to the final four basic needs.

5—Need for Structure and Predictability

In contrast to the need for stimulation there is a parallel need for structure and stability—or a sense that life has some predictable boundaries. A predictable routine can be reassuring when you need a rest from overstimulation or a familiar place to return to at the end of a hectic day. Most people seek a balance between the overintoxication of excitement and the grinding boredom of repetition. Psycho-Logic, however, can sometimes tip this balance too far in one direction or the other. A "don't trust anyone" Evaluation, for example, can lead people on an exciting but frantic search for someone to trust, or push them into a compulsive routine to compensate for the predictability they find missing in relationships.

Nit-Pickers Anonymous

One structure-seeking theme is *Inspector General*. An *Inspector General* compulsively checks, frets, and agonizes over anything or anybody that's out of place, not working properly, thinking correctly, or behaving the way it should. He gets visibly upset over every nick and scratch, or minor deviation from near perfection, and is endlessly scanning dark corners and shelves for unattended dust spots. The first thing an *Inspector General* sees when he enters a room is what's wrong with it. He is uncomfortable with skin blemishes, poor posture, uncombed hair, and children with ice cream faces. He has trouble lending anything because he expects that it won't be returned, or that it will come back with a dent or torn page. He immediately makes a thorough inspection when he does get something back. If you ever cook in an Inspector General's kitchen, you will find him full of "helpful suggestions," like "that other knife is probably better for cheese," or "those crumbs are awfully close to the edge." In the extreme, these Tactics are the basis for the obsessive-compulsive personality.

An *Inspector General* seeks perfection as a way to reassure himself that the world is not as chaotic as it seems, but his circular Psycho-Logic reasoning keeps reinforcing his perception of chaos. The more he tries to fix the world up, the more he focuses on its imperfection, and the more he sees the need for fixing up.

"Inspector General" Psycho-Logic

S. — Survival Assumption.

It's essential for everything to be orderly and predictable (because it was just the opposite in some relationship or at some important time in life).

E. — Evaluation.

Events and relationships are inherently unpredictable (and therefore scary).

T. — Tactics.

Try to make the world more predictable by establishing and insisting on a rigid set of rules and expectations.

Inspector Generals know how things ought to work, and believe that if everyone did things according to their rigid prescription, the world would be a better place in which to live.

Lie Back on the Couch and Tell Me All Your Troubles

A more intellectual gambit for adding structure to experience is *Sigmund Freud* Psycho-Logic. A *Sigmund Freud* is a person who analyzes everything and everybody, searching for hidden motives everywhere. She is always trying to figure out the "real" reason behind someone's behavior. You can see her eyes roll up and left and her head nod as she calculates hidden meaning between the lines of the most mundane conversation. Her own conversation is often punctuated with talk about "feelings," and she is quick to tell you that things are never what they seem. A *Sigmund Freud* considers herself an experienced "people watcher."

Sigmund Freuds usually do well in one-to-one relationships because the intensity they project gives the appearance of sincere interest. Relationships are often one-sided, however, because *Sigmund Freuds* are more comfortable finding out how others feel than they are disclosing their own feelings. *Sigmund Freuds* make good psychiatrists or clinical psychologists, but generally don't do well at cocktail parties, particularly when most of the guests are strangers. Analyzing a large crowd doesn't give them the detailed information they get when they focus on a single person. Unless they can get someone aside at a party, they tend to spend their time exploring "things"—pictures on a wall or books on a shelf. They frequently leave a party as soon as it's socially acceptable, but prefer to be second or third to go so their uneasiness won't be suspected. Still, it can be fascinating to drive home with a *Sigmund Freud* and listen to her insights about individual personalities and party politics.

Sigmund Freud Tactics are calculated to give the impression (both to the user and others) that this is a person in control of relationships. Only she knows how people *really* operate. The more she knows, the more she commands. Nevertheless, the purpose of *Sigmund Freud* Tactics is defense. They are a cover-up for an underlying feeling that relationships are not always in control, as well as an attempt to make them more so.

"Sigmund Freud" Psycho-Logic

S. — Survival Assumption.

It's essential that relationships be predictable.

E. — Evaluation.

When I don't know how they operate, they can hurt me, trick me, or defeat me. The more I know about them, the less danger they represent.

T. — Tactics.

Analyze people. Get them to tell me about themselves without revealing much of myself.

As with all Psycho-Logic, *Sigmund Freud* Tactics can be quite beneficial in moderation. The more intimate knowledge you have of someone, the more potentially rewarding the relationship. But as the need to overanalyze increases, potential involvement merges into cool detachment. A pure observer is not herself a participant. There is a natural tendency to protect oneself from *Sigmund Freud* scrutiny. No one likes to be under a microscope—or on an analyst's couch—too much of the time.

The Three Stooges

Other Tactics for achieving order come from *Manny-Moe-and Me* (MM&M) Psycho-Logic. This involves overidentifying with a specific group or ideology of known structure. When you know who the group is, you know who *you* are. When you know their rules, you know yours.

A *Manny-Moe-and-Me* inevitably feels cheated when the stated rules are violated or circumvented. After all, he joined the group or got into the relationship so he could count on something solid. A woman who defines herself as a traditional wife in a traditional marriage is bound to get upset when she catches her husband running around with one of his female clients—or even flirting with one. When marital Psycho-Logic is based on a Survival Assumption of total fidelity, violating that assumption results in an emotional crisis.

Me, My Wife, and I

George's ideas about marriage were pretty well established by the time he was twenty. One of the first things that attracted him to his future wife was the strong sense of stability she gave him—and the fact that she was *not* into women's lib. He offered a comfortable life, and expected the same from her, but by "comfort" he meant a marital relationship that never changed. Now, whenever his wife passingly considers a new interest or a new girlfriend, George reacts exactly as if she has told him she doesn't love him anymore. From George's Psycho-Logic perspective, love means "not changing" and change means "not loving." When George is threatened with anything different, he has a temper tantrum or pouts for two or three days. If his wife asks what's wrong, he says, "Nothing!" in a tone that implies, "Everything—especially you!" Whenever she shows the mildest sexual interest in another man, George accuses her of being a slut—and he doesn't care how many of their friends are around to hear him. His wife has learned to turn down most party invitations.

George's "Never-Change" Psycho-Logic

S. — Survival Assumption.

It's essential that everything always remain the same.

E. — Evaluation.

I feel so unstable inside that I need an external structure to keep me from collapsing.

T. — Tactics.

1. Evolve a rigid idea about marriage and stubbornly cling to it.
2. Resist any change or threat of change by all emotional means available (temper tantrums, accusations, withdrawal, etc., etc.).

For a *Manny-Mo-and-Me*, the identity group can be as limited as a particular marriage, or as encompassing as Catholicism, Midwest farming, the Anti-Nuke coalition, or American citizenship. It can be a way of defining oneself as a "mother," as a "working woman," as a "macho lover," or as a "college graduate." It is most graphically seen in the insecure adolescent whose acceptance by the gang is the equivalent of self-acceptance. *Manny-Mo-and-Me* can evolve around any external group used to structure the Psycho-Logic boundaries of who you are.

6—Need for Self-Reliance

The need to be supported and cared for by others is counterbalanced by a contrasting need for self-reliance and independence. It's important to have a sense that we are not puppets totally manipulated by someone else's emotional tugs and pulls. We each need a feeling that we generate some personal power to maneuver ourselves in directions of our own choosing, but when our Psycho-Logic moves us too far in an "I'd rather do it myself" direction, we risk cutting too many emotional ties. We try to do too many things by ourselves that simply can't be done alone. This is known as *Lone Ranger* Psycho-Logic.

Kemo Sabe

A *Lone Ranger* wears a mask and rides alone—save for his faithful Indian companion Tonto (who keeps him from bleeding to death when he gets shot up and from going crazy out there alone on the prairie). No one knows the masked man's true identity. He deals in adventures (jobs) rather than relationships that might give his identity away. When a job is over, it's "Hi-ho, Silver away!" leaving everyone to ask, "Who was that masked man anyway?"

A Psycho-Logic *Lone Ranger* frequently finds a faithful, dependent companion in a husband or wife, or a single trusted friend. This "Tonto" (whose own Psycho-Logic is most frequently *Permission to Go to the Bathroom*) keeps the beans on the campfire and loyally follows directions. A *Lone Ranger* rarely has two companions at once. If he trusts his mate (as much as he can trust), he doesn't have another trusted friend. If he has a friend, he keeps his mate at a distance. When a big adventure comes along, he doesn't even trust Tonto, but prefers to meet him at the pass when all the action is over.

Trying to Carry Silver on Your Back, Make Your Own Silver Bullets and Fend Off the Crooks While Your Mask Is Slipping

One of my clients was a thirty-eight-year-old *Lone Ranger* who had worked his way through the University of Chicago doing dishes in the main cafeteria of the Student Union. He told me he had a few casual friends in his Chicago days, but spent most of his time earning honors in management and accounting. When I asked him what he did for fun, he said, "I slept." He was recruited for several teaching jobs before he graduated, but decided to accept a position in the budget and planning division of Xerox. He liked to think of himself as doing his work "a hundred and ten per cent"—precisely what was called for plus a little bit more. He made it a practice to be at his desk before his boss and to stay late, and came in on an occasional Saturday morning to "clean up his desk." When he was moved up to a management position, he became known as a boss who didn't accept mediocrity. His projects were always done on time and done well— primarily because he obsessively checked every production detail and made every minor decision himself. When he realized that a socially acceptable wife was required for further promotion, he found one and married her.

I first saw him just after his fourteenth anniversary, and three years after his last promotion. He told me that he was depressed because he was "stuck in his job, stuck in his marriage, and stuck in his life." After all his sacrifice and all his effort, at the age of thirty-eight, he wasn't happy. He was a falling corporate superstar with no friends and no future. His career wasn't moving because promotions were increasingly dependent on delegating authority and trusting subordinates, and less on handling every detail himself. His marriage was stuck because it had always been a business arrangement with someone he had never bothered to know. It took only a couple of sessions to figure out why his *Lone Ranger* Psycho-Logic wasn't working.

"Lone Ranger" Psycho-Logic

S. — Survival Assumption.

It's important to ride the range alone (i.e., be independent).

E. — Evaluation.

You can't trust the townsfolk or the local sheriff (the only person you can count on is yourself).

T. — Tactics.

1. Wear a mask (don't reveal your true identity).

2. Find Tonto (a subordinate helpmate who follows instructions and doesn't ask too many questions).
3. Deal in adventures (jobs and things) rather than people.

7—Need to Exert Power over Others

The need for self-reliance that we've just examined represents a need to exert power over yourself—to control a piece of your own action. When this need for self-control is turned outward, it becomes a need to exert control over *others*. The most direct Psycho-Logic expression of this need is *Gorilla*.

A Mouse in a Gorilla Suit

The opposite of *Permission to Go to the Bathroom* dependence is *Gorilla* domination—either intellectual, emotional, or physical.

An *Intellectual Gorilla* is a person who always has to have the final word. If you try to have the last word, he'll still be shouting at you after you've closed the door behind you or driven off down the road. An *Intellectual Gorilla* always knows the most, reads the most, and remembers exactly what *Consumer's Report* rates as the best toaster oven. If you have any information to add, he'll always try to top it with something else. An argument with an *Intellectual Gorilla* is never over until you give up in silent frustration. The essential element is not what he knows—even though his information is frequently correct. The Psycho-Logic point is having the last word—not necessarily the right one.

Storing Up Rotten Bananas

An *Emotional Gorilla* pokes around for soft spots in someone's emotional armor, then hammers away at these vulnerabilities until a crack begins to widen—sometimes splitting open an entire relationship.

Emotional Gorillas are especially good at remembering a mistake you made in the fall of 1963, or some dumb thing you said the last time you had your period. If you've told the truth about something that bothers you, he or she will store that information away as ammunition to use against you later.

One twenty-three-year-old secretary, who always had to defend herself against an egotistical older brother and a favored younger sister, developed the following Psycho-Logic:

"Emotional Gorilla" Psycho-Logic

S. — Survival Assumption.

It's essential to attack someone emotionally (before that person attacks you).

E. — Evaluation.

The best emotional defense is emotional offense.

T. — Tactics.

1. Get someone to tell you or show you what bothers him or her.
2. When you feel threatened by that person, use what you know to counterattack, defend yourself or to get even for past grievances.

King Kong

Physical Gorillas dominate by brute strength. Most wife, husband, and child abusers fall into this category. These are men and women who either have short fuses to begin with, or try to tolerate frustration beyond tolerable limits and then blow under the pressure. *Physical Gorillas* frequently grew up in families where parents or siblings used physical force to solve problems or express anger. As adults, they simply pass on what was done to them. Doing what the strong did gives them a feeling of strength.

"Physical Gorilla" Psycho-Logic

S. — Survival Assumption.

Ultimate power comes from physical strength.

E. — Evaluation.

I felt weak when someone beat on me, but I gain strength when I beat on someone else.

T. — Tactics.

When I feel threatened, I strike out.

You're in the Army Now

Top Sergeant is another group of Tactics for gaining control over others. A *Top Sergeant* has little understanding of equality in relationships. To her, people are either leaders or followers. Relationships are based on power, and rank signifies the amount of power available.

Unlike a *Gorilla,* a pure *Top Sergeant* rarely threatens people physically. In fact, she's often gentle and protective toward those she considers subordinate. After all, they are her employees or her family. Nor does she take the trouble to wear people down emotionally or outperform them intellectually. She just gives orders (although she might call them suggestions, advice, company policy, or simply "what's expected"). Her orders, whether they are implied or direct, leave little doubt about the line of authority. She may listen to subordinates, and may occasionally take their advice, as long as the final decision is clearly hers. In most *Top Sergeant*-subordinate relationships, the *Top Sergeant* makes seventy-five percent of the routine decisions, and ninety percent of the major ones. Once decisions are made, however, she may delegate responsibility for carrying them out.

Sergeant Jekyll And Mrs. Hyde

Susan is an example of *Permission to Go to the Bathroom* at the office and *Top Sergeant* at home. Her Psycho-Logic goes like this:

Susan's "Mixed Bag" Psycho-Logic

S. — Survival Assumption.

It's essential to:
1. Have people like me.
2. Be in charge.

E. — Evaluation.

1. If I boss people around at work, they won't like me.
2. My family is supposed to like me even if I do boss them around.

T. — Tactics.

1. *Permission to Go to the Bathroom* at work.
2. *Top Sergeant* at home.

At work Susan feels frustrated and powerless, even though people do seem to like her. At home, her *Top Sergeant* Tactics earn her grudging compliance but very few expressions of love. Until she understands her Psycho-Logic vacillation, she is trapped in an either-or bind that brings her little satisfaction no matter which way she turns.

Tie Me to Your Apron Strings Tonight

Little Mother is another Psycho-Logic method for gaining power over others. *Little Mothers* (they can be either female or male) are constantly on the lookout for stray dogs or stray people—someone or something who appears weaker than they, or as they would put it, "someone who needs me." *Little Mothers* tend to get very involved with their puppy dog foundlings, often to learn belatedly that strays sometimes bite.

Little Mother Tactics can evolve from several Survival Assumptions. For example, if "feeling useful" has survival importance, then taking care of someone might be the motivation for these Psycho-Logic Tactics. If, on the other hand, there is a Survival Assumption about the importance of being strong, *Little Mother* Tactics can be a means of gaining Psycho-Logic strength over someone who seems weaker and more dependent.

One common form of *Little Mother* reasoning centers around the Psycho-Logic notion that you can always depend on someone who depends on you (i.e., you can depend on that person *to* depend on you). This *Little Mother* Psycho-Logic goes like this:

"Stay with Mother" Psycho-Logic

S. — Survival Assumption.

It's essential to have someone you can count on.

E. — Evaluation.

You can't count on independent people. They're always off doing something on their own.

T. — Tactics.

A series of Tactics designed to (a) seek out a dependent person and (b) get that person dependent on *you*.

A *Little Mother* who marries a *Permission to Go to the Bathroom* often develops a mutually gratifying relationship. *Little Mothers* can be quite content advising someone who incessantly seeks advice. The danger in this symbiotic attachment lies in the possibility that the PTGTB might finally grow up, or might latch onto another *Little Mother* who promises even greater devotion.

Little Mothers are generally seen as soft, kindhearted people who are easily taken advantage of. It's a description that secretly pleases them.

8—Need for Accomplishment

What you set out to accomplish in life plays a decisive role in defining the direction your life takes. What you actually accomplish gives you continuing feedback about how far you have moved in that direction and how much further you are likely to go.

Self-Construction

How you judge your accomplishments has a tremendous impact on how you judge yourself. One way to create an external sense of who you are is to define yourself by what you do. This is called *Erector-Set* Psycho-Logic. *Erector-Set* Psycho-Logic is the kind of functional self-definition implied when you ask people who they are, and they respond by telling you what they do. ("I *am* the Vice President in charge of marketing," "the next door neighbor," or "Sally's second cousin.") It's easier and far less threatening to describe "you" as a function than "you" as a person.

In *Erector-Set* Psycho-Logic it is difficult for people to separate their worth as people from their worth as functions. When people are successful at what they do, it brings a sense of comfort and satisfaction, but when they dislike what they do, they dislike themselves. If they feel their work has no value, *they* feel valueless. Even when things are not functioning well, they keep working at it because it's the only way they know that might make them feel better. They have a tendency to dig faster and deeper in an attempt to dig themselves out of a hole.

Erector-Set Psycho-Logic has particularly pronounced effects at certain critical life stages. When a young woman is working on her engineering degree, it's easy for her to envision professional recognition and monetary success emanating from her imaginary creations. When she reaches forty, and her work doesn't match earlier expectations, her *Erector-Set* Psycho-Logic ("I am what I do") can precipitate a lengthy midlife depression. Leonardo Da Vinci—the greatest creative scientist ever known—judged his own life a failure because he left so many projects unfinished. These all-or-nothing failure judgments are a common result of *Erector-Set* Psycho-Logic.

Security for Sale

Once Miriam Wilson understood her Psycho-Logic she could see it was no accident that she was a high-school principal. Community respect and a reliable income had always been a big part of her family's dinner table conversation, especially since much of the family income had to be spent on special nursing care for her Mongoloid brother. Her parents constantly worried about where the money was coming from. When Miriam was eleven, they placed her brother in a state institution. She was old enough to realize they would be putting her away if she had been Mongoloid.

As far back as Miriam could remember, she and her younger sister were given lectures on "economic realities" as part of their Friday night allowance ritual. During the summers, the girls helped run a family vegetable stand as part of what their father called "their contribution." Both girls were expected to put most of their earnings away for college. By the age of eighteen, Miriam had saved nearly $5,000, but by that time her father's "economic reality" had become a permanent part of her own Psycho-Logic.

Miriam chose education as a college major because teachers seemed to be respected and financially secure, but a couple years of teaching left her feeling neither respected nor secure. She raised her Psycho-Logic sights another notch. Eight years after she entered the classroom, she was running the school. She was the principal. It felt as though she had finally arrived.

Miriam's "Erector-Set" Psycho-Logic

S. — Survival Assumption.
I'll always be insecure until I'm financially secure.

E. — Evaluation.

The only way to find stable security is to become a professional.

T. — Tactics.

1. Work hard in college so I can become a teacher.
2. (When teaching doesn't satisfy me), work hard as a teacher (and a politician) to become a principal.

Miriam's Psycho-Logic was working because her work was working. Her security and satisfaction depended on a level of accomplishment that she was actually able to obtain.

Why Do Big Erector Plans Always Come with Small Erector Sets?

Erector-Set Psycho-Logic applies to the mother whose expectations are so high that no child could possibly meet them. Her child's relative deficiencies become her personal failures. *Erector-Set* applies to the would-be tennis champ who loses his grip or finally realizes he never had one, and to the aspiring Valentino whose forty-five-year-old body looks more like Buddy Hackett's. It applies to the sales manager who stakes his personal validation on this year's profits, and to the devoted wife who sees marital success and personal success as synonymous. The inherent danger in *Erector-Set* Psycho-Logic lies in investing too much of yourself in your tangible accomplishments. Careers can fall apart or get off track, and husbands sometimes walk out on Sunday afternoons and never come back.

Hey, Look Me Over

Tactics that at first appear to be part of *Erector-Set* Psycho-Logic sometimes mask a subtle version of *Seal of Approval*. When they do, the emphasis is not so much on what is done as on the recognition obtained from doing it. The specific accomplishment merely serves as a convenient vehicle for eliciting approval.

Disguised Seal of Approval

S. — Survival Assumption.

External approval is essential for self-approval.

E. — Evaluation.

The best way to gain approval is to accomplish something that attracts it.

T. — Tactics.

Create or accomplish something that sticks out enough for people to notice.

A pure *Erector-Set* strategist earns all As in order to think of himself or herself as an A student. A *Seal of Approval* earns As in order to show off his report card. A newly promoted *Seal of Approval* executive enjoys the envy of former peers more than the pride of advancement. A *Seal of Approval* parent wants his kids to make the honor roll so there's no doubt about who's the best parent in the neighborhood. Whatever the specifics, the emotional gratification comes from the applause and approval rather than the particular accomplishment that generates it.

Pointing the Finger Inward

One way to get useful clues about your Psycho-Logic is to take a look at your own needs and Psycho-Logic themes. In the following list, put a check beside those needs or Psycho-Logic themes you think might have some importance for you.

1–Physical Survival
Refrigerator Psycho-Logic (Eating)

2–Need to Be Loved and Cared for
Permission To Go To The Bathroom (PTGTB)
Cute Little Puppy

3–Need for Attention and Approval
Seal of Approval
Flirt
Court Jester

4–Need for Stimulation
James Bond
Tease the Sleeping Dog

5–Need for Structure
The Inspector General
Sigmund Freud
Manny-Moe-and-Me

6–Need for Self-Reliance
Lone Ranger

7–Need to Exert Power over Others
Gorilla
Top Sergeant
Little Mother

8–Need for Accomplishment
Erector Set

Filling in the Details

Using each need or Psycho-Logic theme you checked, see if you can figure out the Survival Assumption, Evaluation, and group of Tactics related to that need or theme.
Descriptive Title of your Psycho-Loogic SET:

"_____ " **Psycho-Logic**

S. — Survival Assumption. (Something you concluded was emotionally important for you to have or to be in order to feel good or worthwhile about yourself.)

E. — Evaluation. (How much of this essential ingredient you had, or how much you thought you could get.)

T. — Tactics. (The specific ways you go about using it, getting it, or compensating for not having it.)

6

Family Effects
on Psycho-Logic:
Finding Your Place
in the Nest

Imagine what it must have been like inside your mother's womb. You were alive, aware, and responsive at least three months before the actual moment of your birth. You alternately kicked, scratched, strained, and relaxed within the confines of your tiny floating world. Nourishment, warmth, and comfort were regulated through intra-uterine feedback from your rapidly developing brain and body. When you were cold a biological thermostat automatically kicked up the temperature. When you were hungry, predigested sustenance flowed through the flexible, cellular connection with your mother. Your only known world was safe, secure, and predictable, but from the instant you were expelled from your embryonic security bubble, everything suddenly changed. From that moment on, you were forced to rely on the good intentions of others to get what you needed—and that complicated your life tremendously.

You quickly learned what you had to do to attract and hold onto this essential human connection. One of the first things you learned was whether you got what you wanted as soon as you wanted it, or whether you had to cry louder and longer to get it. After a few weeks of living with adults, a crude, nonverbal Psycho-Logic was already beginning to emerge ...

S. — Survival Assumption (innate).

It's essential to survive.

E. — Evaluation (first learning).

I can't eat without a nipple in my mouth.

T. — Tactics.

Cry loud and long and someone will eventually feed me.

or ...

T. — Tactics.

Just cry a little and stop. (Someone always comes right away.)

Different Strokes from Different Folks

A parent's unique response to a child springs from his or her own Psycho-Logic. A parent with a Survival Assumption about the "importance of power" will treat a child quite differently from a parent with a high "need to be loved and cared for."

"Need for Power" Parental Psycho-Logic

S. — Survival Assumption.

All relationships are power struggles where winning is essential.

E. — Evaluation.

I must now allow my child to defeat me (and/or) I must teach him to be strong enough to defeat others.

T. — Tactics.

(For raising an infant)
1. Develop a routine for sleeping, playing and eating and insist that he stick to it.
2. Respond to my child when he cries for food or when he is uncomfortable, but not when he is crying for sympathy.
3. Allow him to learn by making mistakes, even if he skins his knee a few times in the process. That just toughens him up.
4. Avoid spoiling him with too much attention.

versus ...

"Need to Be Loved and Cared For" Parental Psycho-Logic

S. — Survival Assumption.

It's essential to be loved and cared for.

E. — Evaluation.

An infant must love her mother or father (to meet the *mother's* or *father's* needs).

T. — Tactics.

1. Spend a great deal of time holding, cuddling, and talking to the baby.
2. Be responsive to the least sign of discomfort.
3. Give the baby all the attention she desires.
4. Provide her with whatever she seems to want whenever she seems to want it.

Getting the Message Across

Your parents' tone of voice and inflection communicated at least as powerful a message as the words they used. "Come here," said in a tone that implies, "I want to be near you," has a totally different impact from "Come here!" that means, "when I speak, you'd better jump!"

Silence can be personalized to mean, "I'm not important enough to be spoken to," or "I *feel* you love me even when you don't say anything." Two children from the same family often interpret silence in totally different ways.

Nonverbal communication—which spoke its subtle message from the time the doctor laid you on your mother's tummy—continued its powerful influence as you grew older. A constant barrage of nonverbal messages reinforced, added to, or contradicted other Psycho-Logic you were learning. It came in all forms ...

The timing and quality of physical affection you got and the means by which you had to "earn" it. (Hugging, touching, sitting on Daddy's lap, pats on the back, good-night kisses, or morning wrestles in bed).

The amount of attention given to you, especially compared to what others received. (Who was prettiest, or smartest, or played the violin the best?)

Whether one person responded to your needs or several people cared for you. (Did Mommy do it all, or did Daddy share the load? How often did brothers or sisters, aunts, uncles or grandparents dry your little bottom or take you for walks?)

How often people smiled at you versus how often they frowned, stared, sulked, or simply ignored you. ("Daddy's tired. Let him sleep." "Mommy's had a hard day. You'll have to forgive her.")

The amount of routine and structure in your life, compared to the amount of surprise and excitement. (Was every weekend the same routine or did weekends become family adventures?)

How much support and encouragement your parents provided. ("You can do it. Just take one step each time.")

How much love was expressed for "being" versus "doing"—and in what ratio. (A pat on the back for being "good" or a pat on the back because you were you?)

How nervous people were around you versus how often they seemed confident and sure of themselves. ("The sky is falling! The sky is falling!" versus "Everything's going to be all right. Just calm down.")

Do as I Say, Not as I Do

Very often a parent wishes his child to directly adopt the parent's Psycho-Logic—to recreate and validate the parent's life view. ("I want my son to be a 'conservative Christian' and/or a 'liberal crusader'.") At the other extreme, there are mothers and fathers who want their child to become what the parent is *not*. These "be-different-from-me" instructions usually involve some Psycho-Logic "failure" about which the parent feels ashamed, embarrassed, or guilty.

"Living Through My Child" (or "Second Chance") Psycho-Logic

S. — Survival Assumption.

It's important to be (wealthy, intelligent, eternally loved, or whatever).

E. — Evaluation.

I failed to be that important thing, but I can teach my child how important it is.

T. — Tactics.

Parental Tactics designed to induce the child to be what the parent is not.

1. The parent's subtle use of himself or herself as a "failure" example of what *not* to do.
2. Verbal instructions for the child to behave in ways that match the desired Psycho-Logic.
3. Discouragement or disapproval for acting, thinking, or feeling in ways that do not point in the desired direction.
4. Buying toys, reading stories, and encouraging the kind of play that fits with parental fantasies.
5. Encouraging hero worship of appropriate models.

Nowhere does action speak louder than words than when a parent actively pushes a child to be something the parent is unable to be. When the parent focuses on a missing strength, the parent's weakness is emphasized by contrast. A parent actually loses influence when the child sees through this ploy to the Psycho-Logic weakness beneath it.

A thirty-year-old junior executive suddenly became depressed three months before a long-awaited promotion. His normally high performance dropped off sharply and his boss received several complaints from one of the firm's largest accounts. This executive was not depressed in spite of imminent success—he was depressed because of it. He was blocking his own promotion because he could not overcome the guilt of his father's death. His father, who had managed a jewelry store for forty-three years, had always considered himself a business failure. He wanted his sons to succeed where he had failed, but the eldest son felt Psycho-Logically guilty for *not* succeeding before his father died. He couldn't bring himself—as he put it—to "build success on my father's grave." Once he uncovered this self-destructive Psycho-Logic, he was free to consider building success on something else.

The Primary Parent

Your parents are never exactly equal—nor is their influence. The Primary Psycho-Logic Parent in your life is that parent who, at any given time, has the greatest impact on your Psycho-Logic. It is not necessarily the parent who spends the most time with you or who gave you the most attention. A parent who is rarely at home may be the Primary Psycho-Logic Parent if the child decides, "Daddy's so important he doesn't have much time for me. I want to be important just like him!" This Evaluation allows the child to excuse his father's absence and, at the same time, turn his own feelings of anger and loss into a positive ambition.

Sometimes a child simply picks the Primary Parent who has already picked him. Sometimes he chooses the parent whose Psycho-Logic is easiest for him to understand or comply with. Sometimes he picks the most powerful parent because he is afraid not to. One study showed that an abused child, when given a choice, usually runs to the parent who abuses him.

The first Primary Parent is usually your mother, since she holds the initial key to survival. But mother and father frequently alternate as Primary Parent as the child's Psycho-Logic needs change or as events—such as the addition of new family members, separation or remarriage—force changes. Occasionally both parents share a fairly equal role as Primary Parent.

By asking yourself, "which parent was it most important for me to please?" you often identify your own Primary Psycho-Logic Parent.* This does not mean that both parents didn't influence you— just that one may have influenced you more.

Family Events

Things that happen in the course of family life can shape or change the Psycho-Logic of its members. Children are especially vulnerable to these events because their Psycho-Logic is not yet solid enough to anchor them through the turbulence of change.

The addition (or loss) of a brother or sister can force realignment, competition, jealousy, or guilt. The accidental death of a sibling who was partly a rival, can leave rivalrous feelings unresolved.

A sudden move to a new neighborhood can cause at least temporary self-doubt if new friends are hard to make—or a surge of confidence if they come easily.

A change in family fortunes can lead a child to expect a pot of gold at the end of every rainbow, or a hole in every pot when you least expect it.

---

*This is not a foolproof test however, since a parent you wanted to "displease" may have helped you develop an angry or retaliatory Psycho-Logic.

The long-term depression or euphoria of a parent can effect the mood of the whole family, or cause certain members to pull away in self-protection.

A change in job or activity that leaves a parent with more or less time to spend with a child leaves the child to determine what that change means to him or her.

Divorce or separation can strengthen or weaken a relationship between a parent and child. A separated father once told me that being alone with his three-year-old daughter brought them much closer together. When she was hurt or needed comforting, Daddy was suddenly the only one she could turn to.

A change in family health—and how a parent deals with it—can teach a child to dwell on misfortune or to appreciate the life and health he or she has.

The normal growth and development of a child can interact with parental Psycho-Logic in ways that are difficult for the child to comprehend. One of my clients expressed her anger and confusion when she remembered how her father abruptly "gave her up" when she was twelve or thirteen. She subsequently reconstructed her father's Psycho-Logic ...

Daddy's "Incestual Panic" Psycho-Logic

S. — Survival Assumption.

It's essential to be in control of relationships.

E. — Evaluation.

I'm in control of most relationships, but not when I'm sexually aroused.

T. — Tactics.

Play with and relate to *little* girls, but stay away from them when they change into women.

If They Kick Me I Must Deserve It.

An adult has a greater capacity to shrug off blame for family events. A child absorbs it.

This tendency to exaggerate his or her own importance is commonly seen in a child who holds himself or herself somehow responsible for the parents' separation.

"Parental Separation" Psycho-Logic

S. — Survival Assumption.

It's essential for Mommy and Daddy to remain together and take care of me the way they always have.

E. — Evaluation.

I must have been bad. After all, they argued about me and punished me. Then they split up.

T. — Tactics.

1. Be perfect so the other one doesn't leave me.
2. Persuade them to get back together. (When that fails) try to get the one I stayed with married off again (in order to reestablish a solid family structure).

Separation disruptions that remain unresolved can sew the seeds for later adult mistrust.

"Don't Trust Anyone" Psycho-Logic

S. — Survival Assumption.

It's important to have stable, consistent relationships.

E. — Evaluation.

There is something about me that drives people away.

T. — Tactics.

Don't give too much of yourself in close relationships, or the other person will take it when he or she goes.

It's not the event itself that shapes the child's Psycho-Logic as much as her Evaluation of it—how she sees herself responsible for causing it and how vulnerable she feels in the aftermath.

Siblings

The first real study on the Psycho-Logic influence of brothers and sisters was Galton's *English Men of Science*, published in 1784. Galton was especially impressed with the large number of firstborns who grew up to be eminent scientists. A hundred years and several hundred studies later, we now know that firstborns far exceeded "both non-firstborns and chance expectation in being Fellows of the Royal

Society; in being sufficiently eminent to appear in the *Dictionary of National Biography;* in being scientists, professors, men of letters, Rhodes scholars; in being listed in Who's Who; in having I.Q.'s in the top 1 percent; and, more recently, in being finalists in National Merit Scholars competition."*

Psychologists now realize that *every position* in the family line has an effect on how that person turns out. Firstborns, for example, are not only higher achievers, but generally more anxious than younger brothers and sisters.

Dethroning the Prince or Princess

When you're used to getting *all* the attention it's hard to suddenly start sharing it. It doesn't matter how often Mommy and Daddy tells you everything's going to be all right. It suddenly isn't all right—and never will be again. When you're a firstborn, the arrival of a younger brother or sister still leaves you number one, but it feels like "number one-half."

Suddenly the new baby's needs take priority. The oldest child feels some sense of loss and betrayal. Her dethroning—no matter how gentle—is likely to create at least some anxiety.

To add insult to injury, the oldest child is not even permitted to hate Baby Joey. She's supposed to *love* him—or at least learn to get along and accept her fate graciously. Sibling rivalry begins in earnest when the oldest child realizes that the fun and excitement of holding a new baby does not make up for the emotional loss her mother never told her about.

"Special Person" Psycho-Logic

S. — Survival Assumption.

It's essential to have Mommy's (or Daddy's) exclusive attention.

E. — Evaluation.

I'm something special because I always get their full attention and *always will.*

---

*From *The Sibling.*

T. — Tactics.
1. Just be beautiful me (attention comes naturally to special people).
2. Achieve things (they give me even more attention when I *do* something special).

A new birth instantly eliminates the exclusive attention clause. Self-evaluations are immediately challenged ("I guess I'm not *automatically* worth *all* the attention"). Tactics begin to focus more on *doing* than *being* ("Maybe if I stand on my head they'll pay more attention to me"). An older child soon learns that she *is better* at most things than her younger rival. She discovers that she can partially regain her position by doing things well and by being a "good girl." After the rug is pulled out from under her once, she never totally recovers. Firstborns tend to be a little anxious most of their lives.

"After the Fall" Psycho-Logic

S. — Survival Assumption.
It's essential to achieve in order to
1. *earn* back Mommy's and Daddy's attention and
2. *prove* to myself that I'm still "number one" (self-approval, like mother's full attention, is no longer free and inexhaustable).

E. — Evaluation.
I can do things to get attention—even though it's now measured out in spoonfuls.

T. — Tactics.
Talk smart, be smart, try harder, build things, play the violin, or whatever.

The View from Number Two

A second child never gets exclusive parental attention and does not set himself up to expect it. Even if a third child comes after him, it just means sharing from a pot that's already divided. He never experiences a devastating attention loss. Achievement is never as important to him because he never loses a favored position he feels obligated to *earn* back. Parents do not attempt as much influence over a second child and so end up not having as much. They are more relaxed with him—more likely to let him develop in his own way and at his own pace.

A second child tends to be more independent, more rebellious, less anxious, and less achievement-oriented than his older brother or sister. When he does excel it is usually in performance skills rather than verbal areas. A second child often sees the intellectual territory as already staked out and looks for a different path to make his own mark. Second borns generally score high on tests of independence and self-reliance.

Second-Born "Independence" Psycho-Logic

S. — Survival Assumption.

It's essential to be self-reliant and independent. (To avoid a direct challenge from older brother or sister.)

E. — Evaluation.

I can make it on my own—in my own way. (Mom and Dad always let me do that.)

T. — Tactics.

Do what I want. Don't be too concerned about what others think.

Onlies

Like most firstborns, onlies are highly achievement-oriented. Even so, they don't actually achieve quite as much. Unlike firstborns, they tend to have high self-esteem and low anxiety—probably because they never experience a sudden loss of attention.

Only boys tend to be more sensitive and easily hurt than boys with brothers or sisters—perhaps because a mother is tempted to overprotect this "special child" at a time when she has no other child to distract her from doing so. There is also an absence of sibling rivalry to model and practice "masculine" aggressiveness.

Extreme overprotection of an only child does not occur as frequently as supposed, although when it does occur, its Psycho-Logic effects can be devastating.

"Pamper Me" Psycho-Logic

Mary Ellen's birth followed two painful miscarriages. Her mother was told not to risk another pregnancy, so she had a hysterectomy instead. Mary Ellen's mother was not about to take any risks with her only daughter. The child was always treated like a delicate porcelain doll—perfectly dressed and perfectly pressed—pampered, hair curled, and protected—a Shirley Temple minus the talent.

Giving of herself was never required of Mary Ellen. Her Psycho-Logic role was to smile and receive. When she grew up she continued to expect preferential treatment. Her relationships with men were a series of disasters. She was perfectly willing to take until they got tired of giving. When they complained, she accused them of selfishness. Her sudden marriage to another only child was a joyless exercise in two people waiting for the other to go first.

In-Betweens

A middle child is often the most confused. He has neither the status of the first born nor the favored position of the youngest. The oldest often forms an "I'll-take-care-of-you" alliance with the youngest—leaving the middle child to fend for himself.

Last Year's Carol Doll

Family position always combines with genetic predispositions and other factors—especially parental influence—to form the eventual Psycho-Logic. Carol was able to see a combination of influences working in her life.

Carol was ten years younger than her older sister Joan and had always played the part of Joan's little "Carol doll" especially after their mother went back to work. Joan and Carol had an unusually close big-sister-little-sister relationship for the first five years of Carol's life, but by the time Joan was fifteen she was getting tired of playing substitute mother, and was more interested in boyfriends and budding sexuality. Carol suddenly found herself losing a nurturing sister—for no sensible reason her five-year-old mind could figure out.

When I met Carol she told me she couldn't trust people—she had trouble getting close to anyone. As she recalled some of her early memories, and figured out the meaning they held for her, she began to piece together the Psycho-Logic on which her inhibitions rested.

Carol's "Fear of Intimacy" Psycho-Logic

S. — Survival Assumption.

It's essential to be loved and cared for.

E. — Evaluation.

I use to be loved but I lost it. (First when my mother pulled away and then when my older sister deserted me.)

T. — Tactics.

Don't get too close to people (or you'll risk losing them too).

Carol was sure there was more to her fear. She had other memories she thought were important.

Ol' Black Joe

Carol remembered childhood visits to a farm her uncle owned. There was a horse there named Ol' Black Joe—with a big white spot over one of his eyes. She especially remembered one weekend visit when she got frightened and fell off Ol' Joe, and her father angrily insisted that she get back up and ride him again. "I felt like crying," she said, "but Dad kept telling me I *wasn't* scared, so I got up again, but I was more scared than ever."

"Why is that memory important?" I asked her.

"Because I was never allowed to cry." After a pause, she added, "Like my big sister was."

As Carol began fitting more of the pieces together, she was able to decipher other messages she had gotten from her father that reinforced her feelings of confusion and self-doubt. Carol finally realized what was wrong. She was not allowed to cry because she was not supposed to be a girl. Joan was "Mommy's girl" and "Mommy's little helper"—and even substitute Mommy when Carol came along. Carol belonged to Daddy, and Daddy wanted a son. After Joan lost interest in playing mother, pleasing Daddy was even more important than ever. Carol became a tomboy and Daddy's "little workshop helper." Everything seemed to be working until, suddenly, it was 1966 and the same thing happened to Carol that had already happened to Joan. Carol had her first menstrual period.

Before 1966, she says, "I was happy. I didn't have to fake it. I knew what to do, but then I woke up one morning and everything was different. It felt as if I was standing on a ladder looking down on myself. I didn't recognize anything. Nothing was natural anymore. I had no recognizable feelings. I had to tell myself to smile before I could actually do it. I couldn't seem to trust *anyone*. I felt cheated."

Carol couldn't pretend she was a boy any more and her father wouldn't love her if she didn't. She was stuck.

Carol's Refined "Intimacy" Psycho-Logic

S. — Survival Assumption.

It's essential to be loved, and intimacy (like I used to have with Joan and then with Daddy) is the only proof that someone loves me.

E. — Evaluation.

I know I'm not lovable because people suddenly stop being intimate with me.

T. — Tactics.

I'll protect myself from rejection by not being intimate with anyone.

Life Goes On—and On, and On, and On

Psycho-Logic lessons don't stop when you leave Mom and Dad, and brother and sister. You take a suitcase full of lessons with you when you pack up to leave, but all kinds of adult events put dents in those lessons and sometimes reshape them altogether.

7

Friends, Lovers, and Events
that Shape Your Psycho-Logic

Lessons from home brand us deeply, but events throughout our lives add to and modify that family mark.

"My father never really taught me how to play baseball. I used to close my eyes so I couldn't see the ball coming. No wonder I never got a run!

"When I was in the fourth grade all the guys used to chose up teams at lunch time. Ronald Mather would pick Richard Grim, and then Johnny—I don't remember his last name— would pick his best friend and so on. The rest of us just stood around hoping we would be picked next, pretending it didn't bother us when we weren't. Then Mather's team would take the field while the rest of the group sat on the bench waiting to bat. The only thing was, I never got chosen. I just backed up against the schoolhouse wall and looked the other way."

The first Psycho-Logic influences come from within the family—from mother and father, brother and sister, and sometimes aunts and uncles or grandparents. When a child turns six, this limited five-room world expands to include a new school, a new teacher every year, and fifteen or twenty other children. How he fits in with his teachers and classmates can help him accept himself or make him feel like digging a hole and covering himself over.

Hattie Reed, a shy sixth grader with a mild speech impediment, wrote this poem for her class assignment ...

No one sees me
In my class.
It's like I are not there.

I go to school
I always pass
But no one seems to care.
Or even likes me much
Or treats me fair
Or says nice things
Or anything.
Except my Mom.
But she don't count
When you're all alone
In that whole mean class
Pretending you're not there.

Playing Another Game

When you look back at who accepted you and who didn't—and what they accepted or rejected you for, you begin to see some of the Psycho-Logic decisions you made. This is exactly what happened to the man who couldn't hit the ball.

"I remember deciding, 'The hell with them. If I can't beat them at ball, I'll beat them in class.' So I was always the teacher's pet after that. I learned how to study and get all As. By the time I got to college everyone was asking *me* what the answer was."

"New Approach" Psycho-Logic

S. — Survival Assumption.

It's essential to be accepted (i.e., approved of).

E. — Evaluation.

I get rejected when I try to compete in physical ways.

T. — Tactics.

Get the teachers' approval and the kids' attention by getting good grades.

Lovable vs. Likable

It didn't take you long to realize that parents were supposed to love you, but that peers and teachers didn't have to. Classmates and teachers judge you at least as much by what you can do as who you happen to be.

School is a time when your competence is tested. For the first time you are forced to compare yourself with a large group of others pretty much like you—and all the same age. The idea begins to sink in that some of these kids really are smarter or more competent than you. You begin to see yourself as the "second worst" baseball player, an "average" speller, or Gloria's "third choice" friend.

If the Psycho-Logic you are learning at home matches what you find at school, your Psycho-Logic is strengthened—although it may undergo a few minor refinements. If previous Tactics fail to gain group acceptance, frustration and anxiety can lead to changes in Tactics or Evaluations, or in the formation of an entirely new Psycho-Logic SET.

Change in Tactics	At home I get a lot of attention just for being me, but at school I have to say something funny to get attention.
Change in Evaluation	Mom and Dad love me but *I'm not lovable* to everyone (i.e. all the kids in school).
Formation of a New Psycho-Logic SET	"Cute Little Puppy" Psycho-Logic works OK at home but "Achievement" Psycho-Logic is more effective at school.

School Lessons

A teacher—who is often the first substitute parent—can play a crucial part in your re-Evaluation. It certainly did for Ben.

Ben was born and raised in a North Shore suburb of Chicago. He still remembered the frozen winds whipping off Lake Michigan blowing across his porch as he and his sister left for school on dark January mornings. Everyone played in the school yard until the bell rang at quarter to nine, then paraded single file through the coat room, hanging scarves and mittens and coats on hooks that were spaced along the corridor wall. If you were last in line you had to squeeze through sideways so you wouldn't leave a trail of fallen coats and mittens.

Ben's fourth grade teacher was Miss Walsh. Ben remembered one particular winter morning when someone stole some of the lunch money Miss Walsh collected every Wednesday. Each child had to leave his or her desk, one at a time, march through the coat room, down the long aisle of swollen coats, and past an empty chair Miss Walsh had set there for the thief to put the stolen money on.

When I asked Ben what the emotional catch was that made him remember this incident, he said, "Being afraid Miss Walsh would think it was me."

This was a very minor incident in Ben's early school life; yet it was one he had remembered all this time—just as if it happened yesterday. What was so important about this memory? It wasn't the story itself. He didn't even remember if the thief was caught or if the money was returned. The meaning for Ben was in the importance of pleasing Miss Walsh—and dozens of other authority figures that followed her. Did this still affect Ben today? Whenever his boss or someone "in charge" looked at him "too long" he became extremely nervous and restless—as if he had made some terrible mistake and they knew about it, "almost as if I still had the stolen lunch money in my pocket and they had x-ray vision."

Was Ben's fear something he had learned from Miss Walsh? Ben never did figure that out completely, but he did have a guess. Ben found it easy to please his father and mother, and got along well with his first few teachers. Miss Walsh was someone Ben had *wanted* to please, but who didn't please easily. That made Ben nervous to begin with. He was afraid that one false move might lose his teacher's approval—maybe for something he hadn't even done. Miss Walsh was the first person Ben tried to please but couldn't. It was something that had never happened to him before—a lesson that was reinforced many times afterward, but which started in the fourth grade.

Ages and Stages

Psycho-Logic that is acquired early and practiced over a number of years forms adult habits that are difficult but not impossible to change. Divorce, death, financial ups and downs, and all kinds of other emotional events have the potential to alter even well-established Psycho-Logic.

Life itself can change your Psycho-Logic. As you grow older, things that were once important gradually take a back seat while things that always seemed way down the road are suddenly on top of you. Each stage of life has a different effect on you because different things are happening to you at each stage. A star-struck teenager doesn't have to face the reality of his limited talent until he's twenty-five or thirty. A twenty-five year old doesn't take her own death seriously until the wrinkles of an older age and the death of her peers make death a waiting reality.

Early Psycho-Logic forms an internal structure with which life events collide. Like a concrete bulkhead, the structure tends to remain generally intact, although the constant pounding of life and fortune inevitably make changes—sometimes undermining the entire foundation.

In *Passages,* Gail Sheehy describes her own midlife crisis which struck several months after she returned from a magazine assignment in Northern Ireland. Near the end of her stay, she was talking quietly to a young Irish boy whan a "steel slug tore into his mouth and ripped up the bridge of his nose and left his face nothing but ground bone meal." Things changed for her after that.

Two months later she thought, "Ireland could be explained simply: Real bullets had threatened my life from the outside. It was an observable event. My fears were appropriate. Now the destructive force was inside me. It was my own event. I could not escape it. Something alien, horrible, unspeakable but undeniable, had begun to inhabit me. My own death."

Common Psycho-Logic forces result from the common experience of various ages. *Passages* is about predictable crises that we all go through at various states of our adult lives, each of which forces a readjustment of our beliefs in the face of some common developmental dilemma. At each stage, we are able to get ourselves together again only after we adopt a new frame of reference that is more appropriate to our changing situation. It is this shift in Psycho-Logic emphasis that ultimately resolves each crisis—whether it is based on our need to establish independence, to merge part of ourselves with another human being, to accept the loss of our youth, or to come to grips with the inevitability of our own death.

Typical Age-Related Survival Assumptions

Ages

0 - 1	It's essential to survive physically.
1 - 3	It's essential to be loved and cared for (primarily by mother).

3 - 5½	It's essential to explore the world (need for stimulation).
5½ - 10	It's essential to be accepted (attention and approval by peers).
10 - 14	It's essential to compete with peers (for grades, beauty, athletic prowess, etc.).
14 - 18	It's essential to be accepted (by the opposite sex).
18 - 25	It's essential to choose a life direction (need for structure).
25 - 40	It's essential to achieve (a happy family, a productive career, creative expression, etc.).
40 - 55	It's essential to accept your limitations.
55 - 65	It's essential to enjoy life right now (need for immediate stimulation and satisfying structure).
65 - 70	It's essential to maintain physical survival, and, at the same time, come to grips with death.

Taking Vows

Marriage, for many people, is their most important adult relationship. The person you care for and come home to every day has a great many opportunities to influence your happiness and sense of well-being. That relationship can affect you in small ways or can profoundly change your entire Psycho-Logic perspective.

An adolescent often creates an imaginary "forever-after" mate who perfectly meets all his Psycho-Logic needs and desires. It's just a matter of waiting until he finds her. No work, just a little patience.

"Glass Slipper" Psycho-Logic

S. — Survival Assumption.

It's essential to find someone who meets all my needs.

E. — Evaluation.

It's just a question of time before that person comes along.

T. — Tactics.

1. Spend a lot of time daydreaming about him or her.
2. Keep my eyes open—we'll recognize each other instantly.

Meeting the Psycho-Logic needs of another human being is not simply a matter of finding the right person—although finding the wrong person can be like trying to mix oil with water. No matter how much you shake them together, they still end up apart. Two people trying to be Psycho-Logic boss or Psycho-Logic leader simply do not mix. One of them either changes Tactics or the relationship dissolves.

One well-known actor, after the breakup of his fourth marriage, described his relationship with his estranged wife as "loving" but "unworkable." "I'm a hundred percent Italian—lots of pasta and pepper sauce in my veins—a lot of wildness. Both her parents were German. She hangs back a lot—tends to be cool and reserved. We just didn't match."

A relationship that does match is "congruent." Each person's Tactics meet the Psycho-Logic needs of the other. If a husband has a need to lead or be protected, his wife has matching Tactics of leadership or protection. If a wife tends to be cool and reserved, her husband's Psycho-Logic doesn't constantly demand intrusion or intimacy.

It is entirely possible for two people to be genuinely in love and still not be able to meet each other's Psycho-Logic needs. You can't give what you don't have. On the other hand, a marital mismatch can meet some of your Psycho-Logic so well that it's worth changing the rest.

Less Is More

Michael and Babs met while they were both studying to become paralegals at Huntsville Junior College. Michael was dating a roommate of Babs and they would talk whenever he came over. Babs admitted to Michael that she had been accepted to a four-year legal school, but didn't think she was smart enough to handle it. By the end of the first semester the roommate moved out and Michael moved in. He married Babs six months later.

No one was more surprised at that turn of events than Babs. Hardly anyone had ever asked her for a date. She saw herself as overweight, and not very attractive. She had often wondered if anyone would *ever* want to marry her—let alone wake up with her every morning. But Michael wasn't that interested in looks. He wanted someone to keep him company and help raise a family. That was pretty much what Babs had always wanted but never really expected. She was lucky and she knew it.

After graduation Michael and Babs worked for three years at the same law firm in Atlanta, and then moved to better-paying jobs in Washington, D.C. By that time Babs had completely turned herself around. She had lost forty-five pounds and was down to a hundred twenty. That was less than she weighed when she was fifteen. Now that she had money of her own, she was able to buy clothes that suited her newly emerging figure. She was doing so well at work that she was seriously thinking of going back to a four-year law school.

When she was asked what had caused all the changes, her answer was immediate—"being married to Michael." After they married, Babs didn't have to worry any more about whether a man would want her. She had one who did, and when Michael didn't bother her about her appearance, she somehow felt freer to take a new look at herself. She no longer had to diet to please a man. With that reason gone, maybe she could do it to please herself. She joined a local health club and started counting calories, but this time she stuck with it. Michael was supportive but mostly left it up to her. As her weight went down, her self-confidence gradually went up. It was the first time in her life she had done something totally for herself—and succeeded at it. Her feeling of accomplishment began to affect her marriage, then her work, her ambition—her self-Evaluation. Michael had always loved her just the way she was, and that had given her the confidence to be something more. She had done it herself, but she knew she wouldn't have if it hadn't been for him.

Getting It or Getting Out

The majority of marriages are based on this general Psycho-Logic ...

"Marital" Psycho-Logic

S. — Survival Assumption.

Whatever Psycho-Logic needs you have that take on Survival importance (need to be cared for, need for power, attention, adventure, etc.)

E. — Evaluation.

I can meet one or more of these needs in marriage (or I can't meet one or more of these needs *without* marriage)

T. — Tactics.

Specific methods for meeting these needs (ask for attention, exercise authority, etc.).

A marriage that does not meet your Psycho-Logic needs relegates a big chunk of your life to frustration and dissatisfaction. Even if your Tactics enable you to fight for your needs, you still lose if you defeat the only person who can meet them.

The Hit-or-Miss of Marital Bliss

A marriage that doesn't work has as much or more Psycho-Logic impact as a marriage that does. When you start out with high hopes and end up five or ten years later with disappointment, it's bound to affect what you think of yourself and what you expect from future relationships. The exact effect of a separation or divorce depends on how the marriage fit your previous Psycho-Logic and how much Psycho-Logic pain or suffering you experienced in the marriage. At the very least you usually go through a period of wondering whether you'll be able to trust anyone again. Some divorced people initially withdraw and lick their wounds, while others glory in their new-found desire to date. Still others immediately begin to scan the horizon for a serious new relationship.

Maggie's divorce three years ago had not disillusioned her in the least. A home and family was still a major part of her Psycho-Logic, but she had learned to be more cautious—her friends would say more critical. She was not one of those women who sat back patiently waiting for things to happen. She was always trying to figure out where to meet people, and who could introduce her to someone who might turn out to be husband number two. Her Tactics—at least up to a certain point—were pretty successful. She had already accepted two proposals of marriage. The latest was Ted.

Ted was living with someone at the time Maggie met him, but he quickly decided that Maggie was the only woman for him. Three months after they met he kicked out his live-in lover and started saving for a Caribbean cruise honeymoon, but by that time Maggie was already having second thoughts. Maybe she and Ted weren't meant for each other after all. For one thing, he was a little too quiet when they talked. She had to do most of the leading. What if they were married and that turned out to be a major flaw? She certainly didn't want to go through a second divorce. Maybe she should put this marriage off for a while.

Maggie's friends saw things a little differently. After all, this was the second time they had been through this with her. Maggie had gotten rid of her first fiancée when she found what seemed like minor "problems" in that relationship, and now she was doing the same thing with Ted. Instead of trying to work things out, she seemed to be looking for excuses to get rid of him, but why would she want to avoid what she was trying so hard to achieve? Maybe because it *was* so important.

Maggie's "Mr. Right" Psycho-Logic

S. — Survival Assumption.

A home and a family are crucial to my happiness.

E. — Evaluation.

I already messed things up once. I can't take *any* chances the second time around.

T. — Tactics.

1. Actively search for "Mr. Right."
2. If I make a mistake and find a man with *any* flaw, get rid of him and look for someone else.

Maggie's Survival Assumption had not changed since high school. A "happy home and family" was as important to her now as it had been then, but divorce had changed her Evaluation and Tactics. She was putting in more effort than ever, but getting fewer results. Maybe her friends were right. Maybe she should try to work things out with Ted. If she couldn't risk a commitment with him, maybe she could never risk one.

Women's Fib

Women's Liberation is not always good for marriage. A dependent girl who starts a marriage with little sense of who she is often grows to be a liberated woman whose Psycho-Logic needs are not met in the marriage. If she already works—as many women do—she doesn't even have to look for a job if she decides to leave. A woman who ends an unsatisfying marriage today has more social permission to see if the Tactics of remaining single work any better.

Women have stopped lying to their husbands—and to themselves. As women's economic and Psycho-Logic options increase, it's more often the man who ends up begging a woman to come back— long after she has any desire or need to do so.

Work as an Adult Event

Children begin to think about what they want to be when they are two or three. By what they want to "be," they mean the work they want to do—as if "being" and "working" were the same. A little girl who wants to be a teacher "just like mommy" or a boy who wants to be a fireman has already incorporated work as something personal about "who I am." An adolescent often selects a career as much on Psycho-Logic image as on substance. When he dreams of being a rock star or a gold medal ice skater he is internally testing a Psycho-Logic strategy for attention, approval, or achievement.

Work Loads

If you are an average adult American, you spend almost a third of your waking life at work. The kind of work you do determines the kind of life you lead. It affects who your friends are, the person you are likely to marry, and what people think of you. It's the main time structure in your life. It tells you what time to go to bed, when to get up, and which socks to put on in the morning. It tells you when you can travel and how long you can stay. It determines what kind of school you can afford to send your children to and whether you drive a Lincoln Continental or a Chevrolet. For many men, and for an increasing number of women, work is a Psycho-Logic yardstick against which personal success or failure is measured.

An insurance salesman once told me he had spent the last year and a half hiding in his office waiting for new customers to call. He had gotten so nervous he couldn't even bring himself to pick up the telephone. He just stared at it, hoping it wouldn't ring. He said he felt like a fool and a failure. Business was down to almost zero. When I asked him about other times when he felt like a failure, he remembered something that happened when he was six or seven.

He was spending the summer at his grandfather's in Scotsdale, Arizona. His grandfather had planted a vegetable garden and carefully shaded it with cheesecloth, which he had staked a few inches off the ground. The grandson remembered tramping holes down the rows of cheesecloth just to see what his footprints would look like—then hiding upstairs under his bed, waiting for his grandfather to come home and punish him. When I asked him how this memory connected with his current failure at work, he said he always carried a sense of impending doom with him—as if he had forgotten to do something but could never remember what it was. He had always felt that way at home—especially when his parents pointed out his failures but never noticed his accomplishments. A report card full of As and Bs was accepted with little comment, but two or three Cs turned into a week-long tirade, and when he finally got out on his own, his parents immediately let him know how they felt about the insurance business. They thought it was beneath him. Even so, his first year was a good one—until he ran out of friends who needed insurance and had to figure out other ways to dig up customers. He never really did. He just couldn't bring himself to approach perfect strangers about insurance. He started going to his office first thing in the morning, closing the door, and hibernating. He forced himself to make contacts only when things really got desperate, but it was never enough. His Evaluation sank with his fading prospects.

When he figured out his "work Psycho-Logic" this is what he discovered ...

"Failure by Default" Psycho-Logic

S. — Survival Assumption.

It's important to be a total success.

E. — Evaluation.

One little mistake and I'm a total failure.

T. — Tactics.

Avoid mistakes (and therefore failures) by doing as little as possible.

With his new understanding, he could see new alternatives: (1) continue to hide and wait to be caught failing—the way his grandfather once caught him under the bed, (2) get out of the insurance business and try something else—using more effective Tactics, (3) hire someone else to go out and stir up prospects while he took over after he had a lead, or (4) develop a radically different Psycho-Logic approach that would give him the confidence to stop hiding. Given his new understanding of the alternatives available, he decided to get out of the insurance business, and to begin taking charge of his life instead of hiding from it.

Illness vs. Wellness

Physical disability, illness, or injury can strengthen your determination or pull the rug out from under you. The age at which an illness or injury occurs has a lot to do with its emotional impact. Losing your breast at the age of twenty-two is a lot different from losing it when you are a grandmother at fifty-eight. If you are born with a physical disability, at least it's something that's always a part of you. You don't have to get used to it suddenly.

Illness or injury has very little to recommend it. Pain hurts and there's no way to run if you lose your legs, but Psycho-Logically it often leads an individual to greater compassion, or it can lead him or her to excel in areas unaffected by the disability.

"Compensation" Psycho-Logic

S. — Survival Assumption.

It's important to _____(achieve, gain attention or whatever the person has learned is Psycho-Logically essential)

E. — Evaluation.

Double my effort in my area of strength to make up for my weakness.

T. — Tactics.

Extra learning, training, motivation, and effort in an area not affected by the injury or illness.

Too often, however, a disability is used as a spiked crutch to manipulate friends, relatives, and caretakers ...

"Helpless" Psycho-Logic

S. — Survival Assumption.

It's important to regain attention or power (I deserve it to make up for what I lost).

E. — Evaluation.

Subtly or blatantly use my illness to manipulate others.

T. — Tactics.

1. Play "helpless" by demanding attention and service.
2. Play on people's sympathy or guilt when they don't attend to me.

Death on the Doorstep

The death of someone who meets important Psycho-Logic needs can dramatically change an individual's Psycho-Logic. Death is sometimes a secret relief from Psycho-Logic guilt or boredom. If it was Psycho-Logically important to please a parent or wife who could never be pleased, the death of that person can end a lifetime of unrewarded effort. If you have been temporarily angry with someone, and that person dies, you may feel guilty that the relationship ended on an angry note. Most often, however, the death of someone close leaves a Psycho-Logic need unfilled. A child's death may leave a mother with no one to care for—or care about. The death of a mate may leave the survivor without the steadying structure of their marriage.

After a period of mourning, an individual may seek out others to fill his Psycho-Logic needs, or he may decide to leave old Psycho-Logic behind in pursuit of new goals or direction. When Franklin D. Roosevelt died, a normally timid Eleanor, who had just begun to step from the shadows of her shyness, fully entered the limelight of her public career. When John F. Kennedy died, Jacquelyn disappeared behind the velvet curtain of wealth and luxury.

Death Watch

In Boston in the Mid-1800's—when a million dollars was really worth a million—Sarah Winchester, the widow of the developer of the

Winchester rifle, inherited $20 million when her young husband suddenly died of an unexplained illness. Soon after, the grieving widow was struck by a second tragedy with the death of her only daughter. Sarah devoted the rest of her life and a considerable amount of her fortune—$5½ million—to the continuous construction of the Winchester mansion, which she vowed would never stop as long as she was alive. What was it that drove Sarah Winchester to spend her life building a house that she would never complete?

After the death of her little girl, a close friend persuaded Sarah to seek the advice of a spiritualist, who informed her that the deaths of her husband and daughter were acts of revenge for all the lives lost with the Winchester rifle, and she was told that the same fate awaited her unless she moved West and built a house for the spirits, on which work would never stop or be completed—and that she would then live forever—as long as construction never ceased.

Sarah Winchester actually lived to be 84—not forever, but a good long time. It was her survival Psycho-Logic, born out of fear and grief, that set her up to prove she would never die as long as work on the mansion continued—and, of course, she proved herself correct. It was not until the day *after* she died that the hammering, and the sawing, and the building stopped.

Sarah's "Immortality" Psycho-Logic
(need for physical survival)

S. — Survival Assumption.

It's essential to remain alive in a fragile world where death can strike without warning.

E. — Evaluation.

When I'm *doing something* I *must be alive.* Therefore, I'll stay alive if I keep doing something.

T. — Tactics.

Continuous construction of the Winchester Mansion.

Sarah's reasoning was exactly backward—it was not the construction that kept her life going, but her living that kept up the construction. But Sarah had a life-and-death investment in seeing it the other way around.

8

Resistance:
What Keeps You from Doing
What You Want to Do?

Psycho-Logic is stubborn. The more you try to change it, the more it tends to resist. It's something like the smoker who notices a cigarette in his hand and says to himself, "These things are killing me!," but shrugs his shoulders and takes another puff. The knowledge that he *should* quit, and even his early morning cough, have absolutely no effect on his ritualistic behavior.

When Freud was first developing his theory of psychoanalysis, he thought that self-understanding would be a breakthrough that would lead to miraculous changes in feeling and behavior. He was disappointed. Not only were his patients highly resistant to self-understanding but, when they got it, it often didn't make any difference. In fact, they frequently forgot their insight by the next session. Freud used the term "resistance" to label this tendency to defend oneself against self-knowledge and self-change. He later found that overcoming resistance was the key to significant improvement.

The "Don't Think" Response

Once a Survival Assumption is adopted, it serves as a psychological yardstick against which past events and future plans are measured, as well as an emotional filter through which current experience is screened and evaluated. It determines here-and-now reactions. When something scares us, it is in our emotional interest to respond immediately, and think about it afterward. This whole process amounts to an instantaneous circuit-breaker protection that spits out a survival conclusion so quickly, we don't have time to think about it. Of course, afterward—when we feel safe again—both the fear and our motivation to examine its source are considerably diminished. We are then back to a protective head-in-the-sand position, since we are not generally prepared to face our irrationality, or to dwell on emotional events that created it. It is easier and less threatening to brush our assumptions off as something we were born with or "just the way we always were."

The price for this "don't think" response comes when we try to survive on assumptions that contradict the reality in which we live. There is inevitable conflict *when inside assumption and outside reality don't match.* We frequently suffer from the physical and emotional effects of this kind of stress, regardless of whether we are willing to examine its cause or not. But, while "not thinking" hurts us in some ways, it also protects us from a difficult, and sometimes painful, reevaluation of what our life is really all about and it provides the security and stability of knowing who we are—or, at least, who we think we are.

Three P's in a Security Pod

The three security functions of Psycho-Logic, or three P's, are Prediction, Protection, and Prescription. Each one provides a powerful reason to keep things just the way they are.

1. Prediction. Psycho-Logic provides a way of organizing and predicting what will happen in the future—from the next minute to the next five years—by making "instant guesses" based on past assumptions. One way we "predict" the future is by labeling ourselves with certain names or attributes that match our experience when we pick them up. These labels then tell us the kind of people we are likely to be in situations still ahead of us.

When a chubby child is constantly called "Fatty Arbuckle" he begins to see himself as reflected in the eyes of the name callers. To have an impact, such a name or label has to contain some element of truth and be stated by someone whose opinion matters. Being called "butterfingers" will seem like a joke to the best ball player in the class but to someone who can't catch a ball, "butterfingers" is difficult to laugh off, especially when he is called that by the prettiest girl in the class.

A label that seems to fit can either reinforce an already existing Psycho-Logic SET ("I knew that's what they thought of me.") or it can form the basis of a new one ("So that's what I am.") Either way, it not only helps an individual predict what others think of him, but solidifies an Evaluation that defines who he is and a group of related Tactics that make his own behavior predictable.

Resistance to change is inevitable because Psycho-Logic survival always feels like *self-survival.* Even when you are aware that your Psycho-Logic contributes to your misery, it is still not easy to change what strikes at the predictable core of who you are. It's not that your suffering is inevitable—it's just that you begin to believe that your suffering *is you. It's important to remember that metamorphosis really does mean killing part of you, but it also means the birth of something new.*

2. Protection. Psycho-Logic also provides protection from certain unpleasantness we would prefer to ignore. Our protective "don't think" response keeps us well insulated from challenges to what we already believe.

Psycho-Logic often "protects" us from dangers that no longer exist. If experience teaches us that the world is a dangerous place, then our Tactics in many situations will be based on self-protection—even when too much self-protection hurts us as much as it protects. It is not difficult to understand why a terrified puppy, who was constantly mistreated, shys away from strangers when it grows up. Early experience teaches the dog to live with the expectation of danger. Of course, some mistreated dogs develop strike-back Tactics. So do some people.

3. Prescriptions. Finally, our Psycho-Logic provides a prescriptive definition of "who we are" by following the premise, "I am what I am because I learned it that way." Once we believe in something, we tend to keep it that way by selectively attending to the evidence which supports it. Evidence to the contrary is simply discounted, distorted, or ignored. It tends to be processed and defined against the stability of what we already know. We actively interpret experience to prove our Psycho-Logic correct. This is like the Jewish mother of *Portnoy's Complaint* who "knows" no one appreciates anything she does. When she buys her son two new shirts—one blue and one yellow—and he tries the blue one on, the mother's only comment is, "So why don't you like the *yellow* one?"

Some people selectively remember NEVER being chosen for the soft ball team because—they assumed—they were NO GOOD at ANYTHING and NOBODY liked them. These recollections support their original "I'm NO GOOD" Evaluation and their subsequent Lone Ranger Tactics.

Selective attention is a very common problem in psychological research. It is very easy to find what you are looking for if you don't set up your experiment to account for that possibility. In everyday life, *we constantly pay more attention to those elements that prove what we already expect.* If you ask someone who tends to be pessimistic how her day went, she will run off a whole list of soap opera tragedies. Someone with a brighter outlook will select a different set of evidence to support a different Psycho-Logic SET.

Indians in China

These three "Ps" describe the three major security functions of Psycho-Logic. Of course, we are not free to select randomly a new personal meaning from every experience we encounter, even though every experience we encounter is unique. Learning *means* applying past experience to present conditions. If we always started fresh, we would always be three-year-old Apaches in the middle of China. Nothing would ever make sense. The old rules would be forever changing and there would be no time to learn new rules before a totally different game began. We couldn't survive, so nobody does it that way.

Instead, our Psycho-Logic gradually emerges from our experience and this, in turn, creates the stability and the meaning of our actual day-to-day living. If it works out that life seems awful and not worth living, then this *is* its meaning to us. If we think life has no meaning, then this conception of emptiness is what it means. There is no such thing as "no meaning." Just because our interpretation of life makes us feel miserable doesn't mean we don't have one—-just that the one we do have is predictably hard for us to live with.

All Psycho-Logic—no matter how destructive it may seem on the surface—serves the functions of prediction, protection, and prescription, and these are three powerful reasons for not giving it up easily.

Split Brain

If Psycho-Logic is such a predictable and a predominant influence in your life, why isn't it more accessible to your understanding? After all, the part of your brain that is doing the running must certainly have some awareness of what is going on.

In addition to the structure and security provided by the "three Ps," there is also a biological mechanism that resists Psycho-Logic change by keeping it out of conscious awareness. The human brain is actually two brains in one; each with its own language and each in charge of its own territory. The two halves communicate with each other through a massive bundle of nerves called the *corpus callosum* (Latin for "thick body"), which constantly passes information between the two hemispheres, and keeps the left up on what the right side is doing and vice versa. When this bundle of nerves is cut—as it sometimes is in cases of severe epilepsy—it is difficult for the brain to function in a unified way. Messages to the two hands, for example—which come from opposite sides of the brain—often compete with each other when the "whole person" is given the task of putting a simple puzzle together. It's fascinating to watch someone literally sit on one of his hands, to keep that hand from screwing things up while the other hand works on a puzzle. (The hands don't always compete, however. The right hand will sometimes help the left hand out when the left hand forgets how to do something.)

Most physical functions—sight, hearing, body movement and so forth—cross over in the brain. If you receive a traumatic injury to the left side of your head, it is the right side of your body that will be affected. The fact that one side of the brain—usually the left—tends to dominate has been known for years. That's what makes most of us right-handed instead of ambidextrous.

Aside from physical functions, most physiologists felt that the two brain halves served parallel functions—that operationally, they were just mirror images of each other. However, in 1981, psychobiologist Roger Sperry received the Nobel Prize for his research that proved this view incorrect. In fact, Sperry and others have shown quite convincingly that the two halves of the brain have very different functions. It is the *left side*—the side that controls the right hand—that tends to be logical, orderly, sequential and, most important, *verbal*. It is the *right side*, on the *other hand*, that tends to be intuitive, creative, visual, emotional, and definitely *not* verbal. In short, different categories of function seem to be handled primarily on one side of the brain or the other—with "verbal" versus "intuitive" accounting for a major functional split. If you need a visual map to follow all of this (as I do), here it is ...

Left Brain Hemisphere	Right Brain Hemisphere
Right body functions	*Left body functions*
Logical	Creative
Orderly	Emotional
Verbal	*Non*verbal

When the two halves of the brain are surgically disconnected, the left brain has to send messages to the verbal apparatus to talk out loud so that the right side can "hear" what the left is thinking. But the right side, which doesn't express itself verbally, has a much harder time communicating back to the left. Normally, both halves communicate *internally*, through the corpus callosum connection, and then translate what the other is saying into their own language. This translation is never exact, of course, since the two sides normally speak *different* languages and have a hard time understanding the rules by which the other operates. This is ordinarily no problem, since one side tends to dominate at any given time, while the other lies back quietly or grumbles but doesn't bother to compete. All of us experience occasional conflict, when the logical side strongly tells us to do one thing while the intuitive, emotional side just as forcibly tells us to do something else. We feel caught in the middle.

Inner Sports

The right brain is the artist and the sculptor in us. It is the half that understands and deals with the language of *images* more directly than with the language of *words*. Since the right brain speaks to us in images, we can speak back to it in the same way.

Adam Smith, the author of *Powers of Mind,* believes that the big mouth, talk-talk-talk left brain automatically shuts down during times when right brain intuition and natural body rhythm are interfered with by all that internal chatter ... when we make our best tennis serve or golf swing, he says,

> What is the click that tells you the shot is good before you know it's good? Maybe that isn't so mysterious. Maybe it's right-brained information that usually gets suppressed by the left brain, but sometimes it gets through before it stops to be translated into words.

> And that total concentration, some psychologists say we crave it almost instinctively, clamping down and focusing and then opening up with a new state of concentration. That's why people take on activities that demand *total attention,* mountain climbing and tobogganing and skiing and car racing, where penalties for nonconcentration are so great that even the language-using mind shuts up for a minute because it understands that at least for a few minutes it better get out of the way.

Self 1 and Self 2

Tim Gallwey, who first developed an inner approach to tennis, and now has an inner approach to skiing, talks about "Self 1" and "Self 2." "Self 1" is that inner voice that's always telling you things to do and how to do them—"Get your racket back," "Keep the ball in front of you,"—or laying it on you when you don't do them—"C'mon Stupid, how could you miss an easy shot like that?" "Self 2," on the other hand, is your instinctive body awareness of how to swing a backhand or traverse a ski slope. "Self 1" is left-brain verbal activity, and "Self 2" is right-brain body intuition.

Theater of the Absurd

What is the psychobiological connection between imagery and emotions? The most obvious is that emotions and images occur on the right side of the brain. This natural connection can be helpful in acting class as well as in the sports arena. When an actor can create a right-brain *image* of the role she's trying to portray, her right-brain *intuition* takes over where mere words leave her performance cold and mechanical. An example is the kind of creative work done by director Lee Strasberg at the famous New York Actor's Studio. One inexperienced actress, who was playing the scene where Salome receives the severed head of John the Baptist, greeted the head with hysterical laugher, her eyes opened wide, and her face and body twisted in bizarre contortions.

When the scene was over, she told Strasberg that she was trying to play Salome as insane, and to show the insanity of her love for John. Before she repeated the scene, Strasberg suggested one change in her mental approach. Instead of a bloody head, he asked her to create in her mind an image of the cutest little puppy she had ever seen and to treat the head as if it were that puppy.

"The second performance was radically different. The servant again entered with the tray, but now the actress responded with childlike glee. Her movements were joyful and excited—they conveyed a sense of anticipation and delight. She lifted the head delicately and lovingly, then gave it a series of short, loving kisses. She fondled and petted the bloody object as she would a puppy. Her actions were neither weird nor histrionic, but they conveyed an awesome and frightening image of insanity." (Shulman, Michael, *Psychology Today*)

The Lie Detector Didn't Lie

What works to focus the mind on the tennis court and on the stage has a lot of implication for use in psychotherapy and mental self-control. Two researchers who looked into this possibility are Reyher and Smeltzer. In 1968, they did an experiment which compared ordinary—and mostly *verbal*— "word association" with a new procedure which they called "free imagery," which was entirely *visual*.

Two groups of subjects were hooked to a polygraph in order to measure their physiological arousal levels. Both groups were presented with a list of anxiety producing words, such as "masturbation," "pregnant," "slaughter," "pain." After one of these words was presented, the subjects in the first group were asked to think of a second word, associated with the one they were given, and to state what the new word was. The subjects in the second group were asked to produce a *visual image* associated with each of the words on the list. The polygraph was keeping its jerky needle track as the subjects responded to the words they were given, and to the words or the images they themselves produced.

The final polygraph results showed a highly significant difference between the physiological arousal of the two groups, *with the image-producing group demonstrating consistently more and longer-lasting emotional arousal than the word-producing group.*

In all, two hypotheses were tested: (1) *visual imagery* would be accompanied by more anxiety than *verbal* association, and (2) an individual's defense mechanisms would be less effective in covering up important problems during free imagery than during verbal free association. Both hypotheses were proven correct. These results gave further support to the growing notion that *imagery has a way of getting to the heart of an emotional matter more quickly and more directly than mere words.* We use words and rationalization to hide our emotions.

Severed Bridges

In another series of experiments, subjects were tested who had the corpus callosum connection between their brain halves severed. Each subject was shown a series of pictures while either the left or the right eye was completely covered. As expected, they had great difficulty naming objects viewed with the right eye. (This information crossed over and passed into the left brain.) When the left eye (right brain) was shown an emotional picture—such as an attractive nude— the subjects smiled or giggled, but when asked why they were smiling usually said, "I don't know." The side of the brain that controls smiling knew very well that something was humorous, even though the side of the brain that does the talking could not identify what it was. Similarly, it is the right brain that controls Psycho-Logic, which the left brain can't always explain or justify, even though it tries.

The Sugar Bird Lady

When you require the right brain to create an image around a particular problem you give the logical left brain a better chance of figuring out what the right brain has on its mind. Very often this right brain image clearly reveals the Psycho-Logic that created it.

"One patient ... described her problem in the first session as having a dominating husband who pushes her around. She was asked to visualize the way she felt about this relationship and saw herself as a little bird being tightly held in a clenched hand. The bird was frightened and helpless and couldn't get away. It was suggested that she imagine the hand opening, and she saw the bird fly away to a nearby branch. She was surprised to note, however, that the bird would not go far away from the hand and that it was a "sugar bird" that fed on sugar provided by humans, having forgotten how to get food for itself in the natural way and, thus, having to depend upon people to live. The patient was able to see through this visualization that she allowed her husband to dominate her because she felt more secure being taken care of as a child." (Crampton, M., *Journal of Humanistic Psychology*)

What was not apparent when this lady described her situation in words became obvious when she presented it as an image. The core of her predicament was not her husband's dominance, as she at first presented it, but her own dependence and helplessness. Her right brain instantly revealed information of which her left brain had not been aware.

Pulling Together

What does all this mean in terms of uncovering and working with your own Psycho-Logic? It means that all the answers are not going to be what you think they are because the most important ones lie on a side of the brain that intuits more than it thinks. Yet armed with this knowledge, you can cross the communication barrier between the two brain halves so that you can begin to function as a harmonious person.

9

Using Memories
to Figure Out
Your Psycho-Logic

Emotional Psycho-Logic is right-brained, yet we try to under-stand it with left-brain words. That's like fighting the right battle on the wrong battlefield. In order to really understand the Psycho-Logic of the right brain, we need to communicate in its own language.

Breaking the Language Barrier

The language of the right brain is not words, but images. It's the creative imagery of the poet, the artist, and the Sugar Bird Lady who understands her need for her husband in the image it presents to her.

Since both emotion and images are on the same side of the brain, early Psycho-Logic lessons are often stored in the form of imagery. If you think of one of your own early memories you will no doubt be immediately aware that it comes to you as a visual image, and *not* in the form of verbal sentences. When you describe it to someone you essentially describe something you "see" or "hear" replaying in your mind. You don't see the letters H-E-L-L-O moving across the bottom of your consciousness like a weather bulletin across a TV screen—you *picture* a specific person in a specific room with specific furniture and, in your imagination, you "hear" someone saying, "Hello." It's as if you were watching an old movie replaying in your consciousness as you describe it to someone.

These visual memories serve as important clues in uncovering your Psycho-Logic because the right brain selectively remembers those events that had the greatest emotional impact. When you think back to a particular period in your life, you don't remember two or three hundred simultaneous events. Your memory takes you back to the specific two or three that capsulize something you learned during that period—something *worth remembering.*

Of all the billions of things that happened to my friend Raymond, one that comes to his mind most readily is a memory of standing before his father, at the age of six or seven, feeling upset in his stomach because he wasn't sure he had correctly translated the words of his summer project. Raymond had fried potato cakes for dinner that night. He knows that because he remembers throwing them up.

Why should this particular five-minute memory stand out among twenty-six years of five-minute events? This memory tells him something about how he acquired his Survival Assumption that the only way to make it in life (and keep your fried potatoes down) is by knowing all there is to know about everything. He remembers this particular theme song because it's the one he heard so many times and the one that still plays in his head at the age of twenty-six. It complements his Sunday morning memory of looking up answers in the encyclopedia before he could return to his father's bed. Raymond remembers finding the answer. Peter remembers giving up without even trying. Peter remembers this so well because he has been failing and getting people to rescue him ever since. The difference between their use of these early memories shows the Psycho-Logic difference between Peter and Raymond.

My client's bitter recollection of watching his classmates chosen for ballgames, while he was totally ignored, showed how early memories pinpoint Psycho-Logic ...

Early Memory:

When both teams were chosen, Ronald Mather's side took to the field and Johnny's team sat down on the bench, waiting for their turn to bat—all except me. I was never chosen. I just tried to blend in with the wall and pretend that I didn't really want to play anyway.

I remember deciding, "The hell with them." If I can't beat them at ball, I'll beat them in class.

Psycho-Logic:

S — It's essential to be accepted (i.e. approved of).

E — I get rejected when I try to compete in physical ways.

T — Get the teacher's approval and the kids' attention by getting good grades.

The Cat in the Bag

Howard "Howie" Timms is a millionaire fourteen times over. He paid cash on the barrel—not checks, cash—for his thirty-three room mansion on Ocean Boulevard in West Palm Beach. He did the same when he bought his sixty-three-foot cabin cruiser with its full-time captain and three-man crew. Howie also rents a year-round suite at a Las Vegas resort hotel, owns a hundred-four-odd pair of shoes—many of which he has never worn since he tried them on for fit—and has his favorite brand of German beer smuggled into the country through the Caribbean Islands to avoid U.S. pasteurization laws.

That's not bad for a guy who barely squeaked through high school, and who spent the first six years of his working life pumping gas. As Howie is fond of telling bare-shouldered girls at Palm Beach cocktail parties, he doesn't know a thing about making money but he does know how to get a cat in a bag. Howard is referring to an early memory he has repeated so often it has become his slogan—almost his battle cry.

He remembers coming home from school on a warm September afternoon when he was only seven or eight. Before his feet hit the second porch step he could hear his mother's voice and other strange noises screeching and screaming from the kitchen in back of the house. A shiver shot through his bones as he entered the front door and crept along the hall toward the kitchen. When he peeked around the corner of the door frame he could see his mother standing on the kitchen table far above him, holding her skirt above her knees with both hands, yelping and hopping in some sort of strange Indian war dance. The family cat was wildly running circles around the table, hissing and screeching as she hit each of the four walls, digging her claws in and scratching across the plaster and down the varnish on the cabinets. Howie instinctively opened his school bag, which was still clutched in his hand, and somehow managed to lunge at the animal when it was off balance in one of the corners. He squeezed the animal's head, and then its squirming body, into the bag and tossed the bag—screeching cat and all—through the back screen door into the yard. Then he fell back exhausted against the kitchen wall and melted down to the floor until his mother climbed off the table and hugged him.

Later they told him the cat had gone berserk. He never knew whether his mother had driven the cat berserk or if it had been the other way around. All he did know was that *he* was the one who got the cat in the bag. He did what no one else would have thought he could do.

Howie never was much for school. He bragged about sliding by tests without ever studying for them. He deliberately gave up spelling in the fourth grade. He always figured he would get a secretary who could spell for him. Of course, no one but Howie thought he would ever have the kind of a job that required a secretary. He started pumping gas part-time during his last two years in high school, and took it up full-time after he graduated. He married his high school sweetheart, moved in with her parents, and kept right on dreaming and scheming while he stashed away as much money as he could from his own salary and from his wife's. It was not until six years later—when he couldn't get a quart of milk after nine in the evening—that he knew what to do. He combined all his savings with a bank loan and money borrowed from his mother-in-law and converted a closed-down filling station into a highway convenience store— "HOWIE'S: Open Six A.M. to Midnight." The year was 1971. Twelve years later, Howie owned and operated twenty-six convenience stores in Delaware, had two dozen more in Maryland and Virginia, and had still more on the drawing board. At the age of thirty-seven he sold out his entire holdings for $14 million, divided his money management among three investment houses, and retired to sailing his cabin cruiser down the inland waterway while he thought about what to do next.

As Howie watches the sun setting over the tidewater marsh, with his feet propped up on his varnished deck railing and a piña colada resting beside his captain's chair, he sometimes tells you with a wry smile, "Life certainly is fascinating!" It's right after that he usually breaks into his cat story.

Weaving Through Your Memory Banks

As you proceeded through *your* own life, events occurred that left their mark on *you*, just as they did on Raymond, Peter, and Howard Timms. It is natural that those events which left the greatest impact will be the easiest for you to recall. You may remember only one specific occasion that represents a lesson learned many other times. Nevertheless, you will find that such memories come to you quite spontaneously, without any real effort on your part. It's more a matter of freeing your mind from distraction than making an effort at recalling anything specific. The importance of those memories may not be immediately clear to you without some detective work, but first things first. You need some clues before you can start investigating their significance.

If you're willing to experiment a little with yourself, one way to begin is to put this book aside for a minute, free yourself from other distractions, relax your mind, and think back to a specific early event that occurred in your life. Take the first one that occurs to you—as far back as you can remember—that you can recall in some detail. You will be scanning your memory banks for something specific that happened on a specific day. On such-and-such a day, such-and-such happened, etc. Try to come up with something as early as the age of five, but at least before the age of ten. The earlier the better.

You will need to reconstruct this event in your memory, exactly as you remember it happening, with as much detail as you can recall—where you were, how old you were, how does the memory begin and how does it end, who was there, what was the day like, what time of day it was, who said what, what everybody did, what you did, what feeling tone you associate with the memory, what part of the memory made you feel that way? You might want to write this story down, or make a list of some of the details, although it's only necessary to have a clear idea of the event in your head.

All this should take you no more than two or three minutes. After you have reconstructed this event in your mind, you will have something specific to sift through as you proceed to figure out what meaning this memory might have for you.

Elementary, My Dear Watson

Now that you have a memory to work with, what you will be looking for is how you appraised it. *What was the hidden message you silently assumed that gave this event its emotional meaning?* What does it tell you about a decision you may have made about yourself, about others, or about life in general? What was the *Psycho-Logic?* Of the billions of things that happened to you in your years of living, why does this particular event, out of all the rest, occur to you at this particular moment? Why do you select this one from an overflowing catalogue of memories? Let's assume for a minute that your mind selected it because it has some special meaning for you.

Now, ask yourself this question—what feeling do you remember having when this event occurred? Do you recall feeling scared, happy, afraid, angry, content, self-satisfied? What is the main thing that happened in the story that gave it its emotional tone? Was the tone of the story emotionally uplifting, or was it a downer? What is the *moral* of this story? *Little boys or little girls who do what, end up getting what?* When you determine the answer to this last question, you may be in touch with one of your Survival Assumptions.

Great Expectations

Early memories give us glimpses of the Psycho-Logic that makes our heroes great and our neighbors human. When we know their important memories, we know something about their Psycho-Logic. (You may want to try your skill at deciphering the specific Psycho-Logic SET behind each of these memories.)

A twenty-three year old school teacher says she wants to be sexually liberated, but is unable to achieve orgasm with anyone but her boyfriend, and then only in one position—her on top. When she's on her back she falls asleep before she gets there.

When she was seven or eight, she remembers being caught masturbating by her older sister who hollered, "Mommy, Mommy! Annie's doing something to herself!" Mother came running, yanked the bedsheet back, caught Annie with her pajama bottoms down, and angrily told her to "go to sleep and don't *ever* do that again." Annie didn't masturbate again until sixteen or seventeen, but soon gave it up because she always fell asleep—lying on her back.

A married man, who is always threatening to "beat the hell" out of his wife, recalls his father advising him "never take any crap off a woman." When he was in the second grade, he remembers listening from his bedroom as his father came home one night, yelling at his mother and accusing her of "running around" with another man. The police came later with whirling sirens, and carried his mother away to the hospital emergency room. After that, the parents' marriage got better and the kids didn't get left with babysitters so much.

What is the connection between the man yelling at his wife, his father's angry advice, and the bedtime memory of his father beating his mother up? *All the pieces of this Psycho-Logic connection are presented to us.*

A young divorcee complains that she "has no feelings" and is afraid she can never genuinely fall in love with anyone. Her parents never punished her, but never touched her with affection either. She remembers sitting in the parlor—just after she started school—thinking of herself as "just another piece of furniture." As these memories come again, she begins to cry.

Brain damaged at birth, a young man grows up unable to walk or control any of the muscles in his body except a few in his head and neck. The only sounds he is able to make are grunts and wild banging of his leg when he becomes frustrated. But his mind is normal—perhaps even superior. The most vivid memory in his life is at the age of ten, when his mother wrapped a mound of surgical tape around the eraser end of a pencil and put it in his mouth. He clearly and legibly wrote the letter "A" on a piece of envelope. The boy is Brian Nichols who grew up to specialize in pen-and-ink and watercolor drawings that sell for a thousand dollars and up.

A rich, pampered, somewhat withdrawn adolescent has a tendency to dominate the few friends he has by planning all their projects and ordering them around. When his mother notices this, she suggests that he be more careful about telling people what to do, especially when they are guests. The boy remembers considering the matter and telling his mother that she misunderstands the situation. "If I didn't give them orders," he tells her, "nothing would happen."

The boy grows up to revamp more of the American governmental system than anyone in the previous hundred years. He is Franklin Delano Roosevelt.

The second son of another Irishman remembers his father's constant admonition that "second best isn't good enough." Yet this shy, illness-prone second son grew up in the shadow of his older brother, who was slated by their wealthy father to become the first "Irish Catholic President of the United States." It was only after his older brother's death that the younger John F. Kennedy was able to don the political mantle himself and fill the vacuum of "first place" left by his brother. "First Place" Psycho-Logic is a big part of what made the Kennedys run.

Itzinu
(It's in You)

Now that you have some idea of how memories can help uncover your Psycho-Logic, you can begin using them to discover some of your Survival Assumptions, Evaluations, and Tactics. You will always tend to recall those memories with the most Psycho-Logic relevance. Since most of us operate eighty percent of our lives from only two or three Psycho-Logic SETs, several memories may lead you to the same Psycho-Logic.

Begin with the first specific memory that occurs to you. Simply recall the sequence of the story in as much detail as possible, and then try to work out the Survival Assumption, Evaluation, and Tactics that go with it. You can either write this down or figure it out in your head, although having it on paper may help you see patterns as they emerge. The format should always be the same ...

T. — The Story.

   With a symbolic title if you can think of one and with as much detail as you can muster.

S. — Survival Assumption.

   What does the story imply about what's important to have or be?

E. — Evaluation.

   Did you personally have that important element in this story, and how did having it or not having it make you feel?

T. — Tactics.

   How did this event affect the way you would run your life or what you would expect from it? What decision or compromise did you make in regard to the Survival Assumption?

The use of early memories to uncover current Psycho-Logic involves the follow-up detective work of pulling them apart and deciphering their meaning. It's Sherlock Holmes solving a mystery by examining threads of evidence. As you deduce the themes and the origins of these emotional lessons, you will better understand the patterns of your life—and how you can begin to control them instead of allowing them to control you.

Cranking Up the Time Machine

If you have now examined two or three of your early memories, you are already picking at the threads of at least one or two of your Psycho-Logic SETs. You have some sense of their origin and the emotional logic that supports them. You may even have begun to piece together how they affect current decisions and relationships.

I sometimes carry around a little notebook or some 3 × 5 file cards on which to jot down memories over the course of a day. After two or three days, I usually end up with a list of ten or twelve specific memories that represent variations of my major Psycho-Logic SETs.

As you acquire your own list you will find you have the ingredients to do some mental cooking of your own.

Leftovers

The following is a list of questions to help stimulate additional memories that chance alone may not reveal. The questions may be used either as a final checklist, after you have already uncovered some of your Psycho-Logic, or as a jumping-off list to jog your memory. In either case, you will not be looking for *general* answers to the questions, but *specific* memories of *specific* events that these questions suggest to you. After each question that seems relevant you should take a moment to see what memories occur to you that are related to it. It's a good idea to write things down as they occur to you; otherwise, you'll tend to lose them. Each memory should have a plot, a cast of characters (one of which should be you), and a beginning, middle, and end. After you recall the details of a particular memory, try to figure out the Psycho-Logic attached to it—that is, attempt to deduce your Survival Assumption, Evaluation, and Tactics, using that memory as your primary piece of evidence.

Psycho-Logic Checklist

Parents

1. Which parent was it most important for you to please, your mother or your father? (Circle one.)

2. Can you recall a specific occurrence or event that you associate with your answer? Briefly describe that event, including as much detail as you can recall.

Using a notebook so you will have as much space as you need, answer the following questions about that parent it was most important for you to please (the one you circled). Label this section of your workbook "Mother" or "Father," or whatever name you called that person. When you are finished figuring out the Psycho-Logic you got from that parent, you may wish to do the same for the other.

1. When you were little, as you saw your mother (father) *then,* (*not* as you see him or her *now*) what kind of *person* was she (he) (strong, weak, stable, demanding, organized, disorganized, quiet, judgmental, patient, impatient, etc.)? What kind of *parent* was he (she) (warm, distant, scary, critical, encouraging, absent, loving, or what)? Can you think of a specific incident in which she (he) expressed that trait or one or more of those attributes? Describe that incident in some detail.

2. How much interest (or affection) did your mother (father) express toward you and how did she (he) show it? What did he (she) think was special about you and what about you irritated her (him)? Can you think of a specific time when that was evident? Describe it.

3. Who was your father's (mother's) secret favorite among the kids? Why *that* person and what did that mean to you? Does a specific memory occur to you in this regard?

4. In what way did you work at getting along with or pleasing (or *trying* to please) your mother (father)? Give an example of a time when you did this.

5. Name two hang-ups your father (mother) had (nobody's perfect), and describe how they affected you.

6. In what way or ways are you like your mother (father) and in what ways are you *un*like her (him)? Give one example of how that part of you is played out in your life or relationships today.

7. What do you wish your father (mother) had done differently? Can you think of a time when that would have really helped?

8. How was the marriage and the relationship between your parents and how did it affect you as you watched it and lived with it? Was there a difference between who *seemed* to be in charge and who

actually was in charge? (Answer this question only once, the first time around.)

Brothers and Sisters—Family Position
(Or what it was like as an "only")

1. What were you like as a child (quiet, outgoing, bright, dumb, athletic, "klutzy," fat, skinny, etc.)? Describe what happened during a particular time when you were very aware of being that way.

2. Which brother or sister was *most* like you (you may have modeled some of your early characteristics after that person, or you may have inspired each other in some way)? *How* were you like that brother or sister? Which brother or sister were you *least* like (or how were you unlike your only brother or sister)? (You may have given up being a certain way because that position was already taken.) How were you different from that brother or sister? Can you think of a story from your life in which these similarities or differences were clearly evident? What happened?

3. Who were the allies and who were the competitors among the children (or in what way did you try to make up for brothers and sisters you didn't have)? With whom did you seem to fit in, and with whom did you not fit? Which brothers or sisters took care of which others and how was this done? Describe a specific example when somebody cared for or rejected you. How did this make you feel? What decisions did you reach about it?

4. What did being the oldest, the youngest, the middlest, or the only get for you—and what did it keep you from getting? Think of an incident that illustrates that and write it down.

5. Beside each of the following characteristics, write your own name or the name of the brother or sister who best represented that characteristic in your family. (If you had no brothers or sisters growing up with you, just circle those characteristics that describe *yourself* as a child, compared to what you thought of as an average child at the time you grew up.)

Smartest	Most Responsible
Most Athletic	Neatest
Best Looking	Most Friends
Most Common Sense	Most Stubborn
Highest Standard of Right and Wrong	Sulked the Most

Most Critical of Others
Most Critical of Self
Shyest
Sensitive—Easily Hurt
Most Withdrawn
Liked to Care for Others
Best Grades
Hardest Worker
Highest Standards of
    Achievement
Most Masculine
Most Feminine
Most Rewarded
Tried to Please Parents the
    Most

Worst Temper
Punished the Most
Demanded His/Her Own
    Way
Openly Rebellious
Inwardly Rebellious
Mischievous
Most Charming
Most Idealistic (Dreamer)
Most Cheerful
Most Materialistic
Best Sense of Humor
Biggest Excitement Seeker

School And Friends

1. When you were a little kid in the neighborhood, how did you fit in with the other kids? (Leader, follower, second in command, one close friend, loner, etc.) Describe something you or your gang did that illustrates the part you played in the group. How did that make you feel?

2. When school began, how did things go for you in the beginning?

3. When did you decide you were dumb, smart, or average, and how did that decision affect you? Think of an example—something that happened, a memory, that this decision reminds you of. Do you still feel the same about yourself today?

4. What kind of grades did you get? Did your grades change at some point from good to bad, or from bad to good? Describe the circumstances (there may be some Psycho-Logic behind that change.)

5. What was the main way you learned to get along with teachers—or to get around them? Describe a time when you used these Tactics. How do you still use them?

6. In what way did you fit in with the other students in junior high (middle) school? Think of a relationship or group of relationships that illustrates this pattern.

7. If your family moved while you were growing up, what effect did that have on your relationship with peers? Can you remember

how you felt just after you moved and the Tactics you used to make new friends?

8. As you were learning about people, what did you discover was the best way to get along with them? As you think back, can you remember one of the early times when you were aware of this? What happened?

9. What kind of people do you like best? In what way does this describe the kind of person *you* are, or in what way does it point out something you lack?

10. How do you fit in with others as an adult? How would you describe your current relationship pattern? Can you think of a time when that helped you and a time when it hurt you?

Physical and Sexual Development

1. When you were growing up, was there anything about your height, weight, physical development, or appearance that bothered you or that you were especially proud of? How did this affect what you thought of yourself? How did it affect your relationship with others (peers)? Can you think of an experience when this physical aspect played a part in your feelings or behavior? Describe that event.

2. Make a brief list of your earliest sexual thoughts or experiences. Describe at least one of them that you think might exemplify some sexual Psycho-Logic.

3. If you masturbated, how did you feel about it?

4. What is the greatest concern you have now about your sexuality or sexual behavior? How far back does this concern go? Describe a specific time when this was a factor.

Adult Experience

1. If you are married, what was the special quality in your husband or wife that first attracted you to him or her? What image did you have of marriage and how has the reality of your husband or wife actually fit that image? Can you recall a specific incident that illustrates your answer?

2. If you are not married, what kind of image do you have of marriage? What image or memory illustrates why you do or do not want to get married?

3. If you have been divorced or separated, what's the most important emotional lesson you learned from that experience? Can you think of a specific situation in which that lesson has affected you?

4. How many children did you want and why did you choose that number? In what ways did you hope children would add to your life and how did you hope to add to theirs? At what times do you feel closest to your child and what times are most frustrating for you?

5. Has there been a death among your family or friends that left you changed in some way? Can you recall something that person once said or did that exemplifies what he or she meant to you?

6. At what points in your life did you change your college major or career goals? What thoughts, events, or series of events led to each change?

7. Can you think of a task, duty, or incident that illustrates how you feel about your career or job?

8. Are there other influences in your adult life that may have had a strong emotional impact? What are they and what Psycho-Logic lessons did they reinforce or teach you?

Putting the Puzzle Together
—And Seeing What You've Got

Even if you answered only some of these questions, your answers should provide a wealth of material from which to deduce your Psycho-Logic. Remember that most of these memories will boil down to two or three Psycho-Logic SETs that repeat themselves in many variations. There is evidence that when your Psycho-Logic changes, your right brain selects new memories that support the new Psycho-Logic. What you remember *right now* tells you the Psycho-Logic you are operating under *right now.* Choices begin to open up in front of you when you stop pretending and defending and take a closer look at what's really going on—and why it is.

The Bliss and Miss of Ignorance

It is only a knowledge of your Psycho-Logic and how it functions that can keep it from malfunctioning. The less you understand it, the more it controls you, and the more you end up suffering the consequences—whatever they may be. The more you understand your Psycho-Logic, the more choice you have about it—even if the choice is simply to leave it alone. The parts that are not working for you, you can *choose* to change—and you can even add totally new Psycho-Logic that works in ways not previously within your grasp.

10

Taking Charge
of Your Life

In *Camelot,* King Pellinore stumbles right into the middle of Guinevere's garden scene, with his flop-down helmet and bulge-belly armor, demanding to know if anyone has seen the beast he's been chasing for the past forty years. Pellinore has never seen the beast himself, but he has heard it has the body of a boar, the tail of a lion, and the head of a snake.

At one point in the play, King Arthur, who is having his own love problems, asks Pellinore if he's ever been married.

"Oh, no," answers Pelli. "Been too busy chasing the beast."

Chasing the beast is the Psycho-Logic that drives Pellinore's life. It directs his thinking, guides his action, structures his experience, colors his perspective, tunnels his vision, and gives him something to pursue.

When we started looking for the reasons each of us pursues particular phantoms in life, we found that a good deal of it has to do with the small set of Survival Assumptions. These assumptions are established at a time when we are trying to figure out what life is all about, and how we are going to Psycho-Logically survive in a world of power giants, limited attention, and competition all around. We didn't always figure it out correctly, but we did figure out something, and that something formed the basis of what life *seemed* like to us.

A personal and unique Psycho-Logic evolved around three or four major Survival Assumptions. Subsequent decisions based on these assumptions further established their validity and reinforced their habit power.

Once you figure out this personal Psycho-Logic, you will be able to judge whether it's a beast worth chasing or whether it simply distracts you from more satisfying pursuits. You will be able to determine which components of your Psycho-Logic are working for your benefit and which are holding you back. In any given situation, you will be able to ask yourself, "Does this Psycho-Logic enhance or interfere with my personal effectiveness, joy, or satisfaction?" Your answer may help you decide that particular changes are called for in some of your Tactics, one or more of your self-Evaluations, or even in a Survival Assumption. Remember, though, that Psycho-Logic is built in what *feels* like a logical sequence—if A is true and B follows, then C is the result. A change in any one of these components is likely to have at least some effect on the others.

Catch 22

Each component of a Psycho-Logic SET tends to lock the others in place. It's difficult to make an isolated change in external Tactics (such as disclosing more of yourself) without challenging the internal rationale that supports this behavior (your fear of setting yourself up for another rejection). Looking at it the other way around, it's difficult to overcome an internal fear of rejection without taking the external risk of disclosing yourself. When you try to tackle either the internal or the external alone, the other gives you an instant excuse for not changing. Your fear of rejection keeps you from engaging in disclosure Tactics, and not engaging in the Tactics of disclosure keeps the fear alive—Catch 22.

What if Carol, for example, decided to make a change in only one component of her Intimacy Psycho-Logic?

Carol's "Intimacy" Psycho-Logic

S. — Survival Assumption.

    1. It's essential to be loved.

    2. Intimacy is the only proof that someone loves you.

E. — Evaluation.

    Since I'm not lovable, no one wants to be intimate with me.

T. — Tactic.

    I'll protect myself from rejection by not being intimate.

Carol could alter her protectionistic Tactics by disclosing more of her feelings, but her intense fear of rejection would almost certainly cause her a great deal of anxiety. On the other hand, she could change her "I'm not lovable" Evaluation, but this would be difficult without concrete evidence that she is in fact lovable. She could try to change one or both of her Survival Assumptions, but Survival Assumptions touch the heart of who she thinks she is, and attempting to destroy the core of her personal meaning would feel like the equivalent of emotional suicide.

Mismatches

Occasionally a change in one Psycho-Logic component does occur without a corresponding change in the others. When this does happen, it can leave the individual with incongruent Tactics that have no personal meaning, or with a Survival Assumption and Evaluation that have no means of expression. This is an occupational hazard of the businessman whose self-Evaluation has been ground down by the toil of thirty years on the job, leaving him with worn-out Tactics that no longer fit anything that seems important. The usual result is drudgery, despondency, and emotional withdrawal.

In Carol's case, if she were finally able to be intimate with someone but *still* Evaluated herself as "unlovable" she would certainly feel like giving up her effort. Or if she somehow re-Evaluated herself as "lovable" but had no way of allowing others to express their love for her, she would continue to experience rejection.

Any meaningful change in Psycho-Logic must ultimately involve internal *and* external change. The most effective way to challenge automatic Psycho-Logic is to deliberately implement an alternative Counter Logic that simultaneously deals with how you feel and how you act.

Structured Alternatives

The first step in getting on a more productive Psycho-Logic track is knowing what your Psycho-Logic is and how it operates. The second step is the deliberate creation of a more effective Counter-Logic alternative.

In contrast to the three components of a Psycho-Logic SET, there are only two components to Counter Logic—the Counter Logic itself and the Counter Tactics.

Counter Logic

Counter Logic	A new internal perspective that is factual, simple and potentially more effective than the Survival Assumption or Evaluation it is intended to replace.
Counter Tactics	Specific actions that plug the new Counter Logic into your life.

Counter Logic, by necessity, must be incompatible with the Psycho-Logic it is intended to replace. If your Psycho-Logic Tactics require you to stand up, your Counter Logic Tactics should involve sitting down. If you Evaluate yourself as unlovable, your Counter Logic should suggest that you *are* lovable. When you are implementing your Counter Logic, you should be automatically weakening your Psycho-Logic.

Carol, for example, might use the Counter Logic, "No one gets loved *all* the time." The very formulation of this Counter Logic might strike her as humorous since it points the finger at the magical expectation she secretly harbors. If she were able to see things from this new and more realistic perspective she might relax enough to risk some rejection in order to gain some acceptance. The Counter Tactics of *selective* intimacy might naturally flow from such Counter Logic. She might be able to develop the courage to take small risks under conditions that could lead to reciprocation.

Carol's "Self-Disclosure" Counter Logic

Counter Logic	"No one gets loved *all* the time."
Counter Tactics	1. Be more superficially friendly to more people (smile, say "hello," remember people's names). 2. Ask leading questions *only* of those who reciprocate (who smile back and remember my name). 3. Disclose a little more about me *when* and *if* they disclose a little more about them.

Characteristics of Counter Logic

Once a decision has been made to challenge a Psycho-Logic SET, an internal change will be easiest to accomplish if the proposed Counter Logic meets the following four-point test.

Test 1—It must be true, to the best of your knowledge, based on a full understanding of your choices at this point in your life. You will be developing Counter Logic you would *like* to put into practice, but which is not now your ordinary way of seeing things. It is essential that this Counter Logic ring true when you say it to yourself. It is not likely that you will be able to challenge life-long Psycho-Logic with something that isn't even intellectually believable.

Test 2—It must be worded simply so that an average six-year-old could immediately grasp its meaning. Remember, Psycho-Logic reactions occur instantaneously. When you need a quick Counter-Logic alternative you don't have time to recite a Shakespearean sonnet. You need something with immediate power that contains the essence of what you're trying to internalize.

Test 3—It must be a positive statement. It should state the way you *do* want to look at something and the way you *do* want to behave, rather than the way you shouldn't think or behave.

Test 4—It must touch your emotions. It should be a catchy self-advertising phrase such as, "Reach out and touch someone." Madison Avenue is well aware of the benefits of associating happiness, excitement, and beautiful people with commercial products. Look at the "cola generation" ads, or "a smile-and-a-cola"—one sided views of life, but still partially real. These ads are a joy to watch because they are emotionally catchy. The cola ad men create emotional language and imagery around which good feelings naturally flow. You can use this same kind of emotional phrasing to propagandize yourself in positive directions.

Death in the Family

We have already seen that life events can profoundly affect Psycho-Logic, but not usually in a planned or controlled way. Simply getting older gradually changes a person's view of himself and what he or she wants or expects from life. The death of someone Psycho-

Logically important can alter a person's Psycho-Logic suddenly and drastically.

Suppose a devoted mother operated from this Psycho-Logic:

S. — Survival Assumption.

It's essential to love and care for someone (in order for me to have any significance).

E. — Evaluation.

My son is the only one who accepts my love and caring.

T. — Tactic.

Cooking, cleaning, caring, and worrying about my son.

If this woman's son were to die, her Psycho-Logic might suddenly change to this:

S. — Survival Assumption.

It's essential to love and care for someone (in order for me to have any significance).

E. — Evaluation.

My son *used to be* the only one who accepted my love and caring. Now no one does.

T. — Tactics.

1. Refuse to accept the death of my son.
2. Put my own life on indefinite hold.

How could such a woman regain control of her life after this tragic loss and find the courage to look for meaning in some other direction? How could any simple phrase—or anything that anyone could say—help her get beyond her suffering? These are the kinds of difficult questions that frequently confront a psychotherapist.

Yellow Ribbons

A beautiful, but tragic example of Counter-Logic effectiveness was presented on *60 Minutes* several years ago. A woman's only child—her twelve-year-old son—had died in an auto accident and the woman had spent the next year visiting the cemetery every morning and placing daffodils at the foot of the grave. The boy's room at home was left unchanged—untouched. The door was simply closed as if time had frozen. The mother's life came to a stop. She quit her job and just sat staring at the TV, feeling empty, abandoned, and useless. She was given antidepressants but she still sat—sometimes crying, but mostly just staring blankly, with little sign of emotion.

When nothing else worked, she was sent to a psychologist in the Netherlands who had gained a reputation for relieving intransigent depression. This time, the *60 Minutes* camera crew went along to film the treatment. What was eventually shown on television was a twenty minute condensation of what happened over ten days of daily treatment.

The first couple of days, the woman looked awful. She wore a plain housedress; her hair was combed, but had no style to it, and she had on no makeup. She sat slumped limply in her chair, expressionless, avoiding eye contact with either the psychologist or the camera. There was a great deal of silence. She volunteered almost nothing, but sometimes cried when the psychologist asked her how she felt—or she would just look at the floor and ask, "Who cares?"

It was a couple of days before she could bring herself to describe the auto accident. Later, she was able to discuss some of her feelings about her dead son—why having a child had been so central to her Psycho-Logic, and what her relationship with him had meant. She said there was a song he had liked—"Tie A Yellow Ribbon 'Round the Old Oak Tree"—that they still played on the radio sometimes—but she couldn't bear to listen to it anymore. She had hidden all his pictures in a drawer because she couldn't bring herself to face them.

Throughout the early sessions, the psychologist began softly but persistently presenting her with the new reality she didn't want to face. When she was telling something about her son, and there was a natural pause, he would say quietly, "He's dead now," and then wait. The woman would stop—sometimes she would cry. After a while, he might repeat, "He's dead now," or he might wait for the woman to go on, and then repeat this harsh reality again later.

By the fifth or sixth day, the woman was able to bring in a picture of her son. He began encouraging her to hold it up and look at it. When she was finally able to face it squarely, without resisting, he said, "It's hard to believe, as you look at those sad, beautiful eyes, that he's dead now." She cried and turned the picture over in her lap.

It was no longer possible for her to avoid what she had so carefully avoided for a year. As each day passed, she was forced to face what she could not bear. By the eighth session, he had her closing her eyes and trying to picture vividly the face of her son, as if he were sitting right there in front of her. Now the psychologist added an additional Counter Logic phrase—"He's dead now. *Let him go.*" The woman said nothing, but shook her head. "No." He repeated it, "He's dead now. *Let him go.*"

By the ninth session, not much had changed for the woman—she looked the same, her feeling tone was the same. Half an hour of that session had gone by before he said it again, *"Let him go."* There was a long pause this time, but no crying. The woman took a deep, labored breath, and breathed out a sigh of relief. The session was ended and she got up and left.

When she returned for the tenth and final session, things were totally different. She wore a bright stylish dress, had fixed her hair up, and had bought some new makeup which she obviously knew how to use. She was smiling for the first time.

The psychologist said he wanted her to hear something. He punched the "Play" button on a small tape recorder, and Tony Orlando started singing, "Tie a Yellow Ribbon 'Round the Old Oak Tree. It's been three long years. Do you still want me?" The woman kept smiling. When the song was over she said she felt fine. That song brought back good memories now. She could live with these memories and wouldn't have to fight them any more.

Counter Logic that Hits Home

One of the reasons this approach worked so well was that it met the four-point test for effective Counter Logic. "Let him go," was certainly a *true* representation of exactly what this woman needed to accept. It was *worded simply.* It was a *positive statement* of something with which she needed to come to grips, and it was phrased in a way that *touched the emotional core* of her original Psycho-Logic. Accepting this death as a fact of life was still not easy, but at least it matched her current reality better than the one that had died with her son.

Directed Counter Logic

If we have an outdated beauty assumption it will never bring us satisfaction no matter how stubbornly we cling to it. Our energies might be more fruitfully applied toward changing our Psycho-Logic into something that does work. But what kind of Counter Logic might effectively challenge beauty Psycho-Logic that isn't working?

Ineffective "Beauty" Psycho-Logic

S. — Survival Assumptions.

It's important to be beautiful because my older sister was.

E. — Evaluation.

I'm not beautiful.

T. — Tactic.

Doing well in school and being smart will make up for not being beautiful.

At the age of 35, this successful college professional was still not satisfied with herself. No matter how smart or how successful she became, she was still not what she *really* wanted to be.

In examining her Psycho-Logic she concluded that the only part of it that was objectively correct was her Evaluation—she was definitely *not* beautiful. She had tied her success to a physical impossibility that guaranteed constant disappointment. Her Tactics made her superficially successful, but her success did not measure up to her own Psycho-Logic criteria—a beautiful face and body.

After examining this Psycho-Logic dilemma, she concluded that the only way out was to directly challenge her "important-to-be-beautiful" Survival Assumption, but what Counter Logic could she use to challenge it? She began the process of renewed reasoning and dialogue with herself.

"It's essential to be beautiiful!"

"Essential for what?"

"Happiness."

"My sister was beautiful. Is she happy?"

"She certainly was a happy child—with all that attention. But she doesn't seem to be so happy lately. My God, she's thirty-seven and must be afraid of losing everything!"

With this woman's Psycho-Logic out in the open, picking it apart was easier than she had expected.

"Is every beautiful person happy?"

"Of course not."

"Are there at least some happy people who aren't beautiful?"

"Of course."

Her self-questioning continued.

"If I could be happy but not beautiful, which would I choose?"

"Happy, of course."

"But I always thought they went together."

"That was a five-year-old decision. I don't think that now, but how do I persuade myself to *feel* differently?"

Another dialogue—

"Why do I want to be beautiful?"

"Because my sister was."

"And what did it get her that I wanted?"

"All that attention."

"So it's the attention I really wanted. Beauty was just the most obvious means of getting it!"

This was an insight she hadn't thought of before. She decided to use it as a basis for her Counter Logic.

"Extra Attention" Counter Logic

CL   It's important to get attention.

CT

1. Start to enjoy the attention I'm already getting for being smart (who cares what it's for!).
2. Find new ways of getting attention that make some satisfying contribution (such as doing more research or publishing useful articles).
3. Develop relationships that give me attention for the person I am instead of the person I dreamed up.

At first a decision to change from a Survival Assumption based on beauty to one based on attention struck her as a little immature, but at least it seemed achievable—and potentially more satisfying. That felt like a big improvement over what she had.

Blossoming Beauty

What if the woman in question had been unattractive as a child but had blossomed at seventeen or eighteen? Her Psycho-Logic Evaluation may not have changed with her figure. Under these circumstances the best approach might be a Counter Logic attack against her incorrect Evaluation.

"Ugly Duckling" Counter Logic

CL   The ugly duckling turned into a beautiful swan. Maybe I did too.

CT
1. Take a closer look at my *new* self in the mirror.
2. Start buying clothes, applying makeup and treating myself *as if* I were attractive.
3. Become more attuned to feedback I get from others—especially what they say about me when they don't think I'm listening.
4. Ask for *honest* feedback from someone I trust, and give that person permission to tell me the truth.

Trying New Tacks

If Raymond reached a point in his life when achievement alone was no longer fully satisfying, he might wish to revise, at least slightly, his achievement Psycho-Logic. An effective use of Counter Logic might move him toward potentially satisfying realms he has not yet explored.

"New Adventure" Counter Logic

CL   "There's more to life than achievement."

CT
1. Regain the wonder of a rainy day (i.e., the sensual pleasure of direct experience).
2. Get to know my family more intimately.
3. Read three books a year just for fun.
4. Take vacation on which I don't try to learn anything.
5. Allow my sexual partner to give *me* pleasure.

Little Peter's "successful failure" Psycho-Logic would require more extensive Counter Logic surgery. He would need to directly challenge his Survival Assumption that extraordinary achievement was the *only* way to feel good about himself. This would a difficult task, but one that might be finally worth achieving.

I.M.I.

David Wexler describes self-actualization—or continued self-growth—as "the degree to which a person characteristically engages in a mode of information processing in which he is his *own source* (italics mine) for creating new experience. The operations involved in this mode of information processing are intimately related to man's unique ability to symbolize; a person in the ongoing process of organizing diverse and complex information in his life can create new experience and change himself by continually distinguishing new facets of meaning in his information."

We free ourselves to create new meaning from experience as soon as we perceive that we have new information or *have a new way of dealing with the old*. Counter Logic is a structured method for processing information that puts one at the center of his own creative experience and—even more important—at the center of what it symbolically means to him. In the end, inner freedom does not come from existence without structure, but rather from a decision to be an architect instead of a maintenance man.

11

Using Images
as Guides

Images play an essential part in our mental lives. We dream them up every night, and constantly watch them flash through our daytime awareness. Since they come from the same side of the brain as our emotions, they can help us understand our emotions better and provide a method for direct emotional influence. Directed images can be used to challenge Psycho-Logic in the same way verbal Counter Logic is used. Instead of constructing alternative *verbal* perspective, you simply construct an alternative *visual image* to accomplish the same purpose. If you are dieting, for example, instead of saying to yourself, "Count your calories," or "One mouthful at a time," you might visualize what you will look like when you achieve the tanned bikinied body you are working toward. If you focus on this image at the crucial moment of eating it can help you choose a thin body over that bite you're about to stick in your mouth.

A Magical Mystery Tour of the Mind

I would like you to try a two-minute experiment in image control. It is a simple exercise, but one I think will demonstrate effects these images can have on you. As you read through this, keep in mind that you gain a little from just reading about it, but you can gain the actual experience only by participating in it.

There are three parts to this exercise. Each takes less than a minute. The best approach is to read one section at a time, then follow those instructions before moving on.

1. First, I would like you to sit back, relax, and get as comfortable as you can. Take a few seconds to do this.

Now let your mind quietly float back to some specific time and place in your life when you felt happy, content, and at ease with yourself. This may have been a vacation in the country or at the beach—or it may have been just lying in the grass watching the summer clouds float by, or sitting by the warmth of a crackling fire on a cool autumn evening—any pleasant, *specific* memory will do. Take a moment now to let your mind recall one.

Now I would like you to relax even further—let all the remaining tension flow from your body. Then gently close your eyes and try to revisualize that place and that time, recreating as much sensual detail as you can. Try to rehear those same sounds, smell that aroma again, feel that warmth or coolness brush against your skin once more, and put yourself back in the middle of those physical surroundings. Notice the time of day and how the light and shadows fall on the objects you see. Notice the colors. This may take you a minute or so to accomplish. There is no need to rush. You'll know when you have it clearly.

When you feel you have *immersed* yourself in the physical sensation of this memory, I would like you to recapture—actually *reexperience* the emotional feelings of warmth and comfort that led you back to this memory. Take a few seconds to sense the freedom you find in these feelings of relaxation and ease. Feel them all over again *right now.* Put yourself back there and enjoy those same feelings again.

When you have completed this part of the experiment to your satisfaction, you are ready to go on with Part 2.

2. Now I would like you to select another memory from a time when you felt disappointed, upset, frightened, or very angry at a particular person or situation. Take a moment to recall that memory now.

Again, I would like you to close your eyes and recreate that memory in your imagination—starting with the physical surroundings and sensations that go with it—the sights (the room, beach, trees, sun, etc.), sounds (people talking or yelling, what they are saying, tone of voice, cars crashing, noise or silence, etc.), aroma (if any), and touch (physical pain, skin against skin, the emptiness of no touch at all, etc.). If a snake was a part of this experience, don't think snake—*see and feel that snake* again in your mind. Put yourself there instead of here. When these physical sensations are clear again in your mind—and this is an essential step—turn your attention to the *feelings* of fear or horror, or discouragement, or anger that brought you back to this memory. *Reexperience* them. Feel in your mind and body what your mind and body felt then.

When you are satisfied you have accomplished this, you are ready for the third and final part of the experiment.

3. Now I would like you to close your eyes once more and *visualize* the burning flame of a candle in the middle of a very dark room. There is only enough light to see the upper half of the candle and the gentle dance of the flame as it flickers in front of your eyes.

When this image is clear to you, concentrate on the flame of the candle for as long as you can without allowing *any other thought* to enter your mind. If another thought does enter, simply make note of it, and refocus your attention on the flame. Try not to allow any further thoughts to interrupt your concentration for the next minute or so. When the time is up, this part of the experiment is complete.

Who's in Charge

What does this experiment demonstrate? First, I hope it demonstrates—at least to some extent—that your mind will follow its own instructions, and that you can target images in preselected directions. Second, it is intended to isolate the frequent connection between the contents of your mind and their effect on how you feel.

Neither of the two memories you selected were anything *currently* real—both were recreated images. They weren't even in your mind until you *chose* to put them there. Of course, the words in this book instructed you to do so, but you could have ignored these instructions—and probably did ignore at least some of them. No one instructed you to read the instructions. Certainly no one chose the particular memories that occurred to you. You controlled only a specific memory *category* by your internal directions to select a relaxing memory or an uncomfortable one, but that was enough to significantly affect—and change—how you feel RIGHT NOW. The point is, there were *two* sets of feelings—one that occurred with the actual event, and another that just now occurred with your memory of it. If you had not followed the instructions, this second set of feelings would not have occurred at this particular moment in your life.

Drunken Monkeys

How did you do with the "candle image" experiment? Even a Tibetan Lama, trained in the ancient art of Hindu meditation, would have had trouble following those instructions for any length of time. The mind just isn't capable of concentrating on any single thought for more than a few seconds. In fact, the point of the experiment was to demonstrate how fickle human concentration is—that random thoughts and images enter the mind constantly, and that they are only marginally within the realm of your control. In the few minutes it has taken me to write this paragraph, I have caught myself thinking about lunch, the mismatch between my navy blue socks and the lighter blue in my jeans, a slight ringing in my left ear, an overdue library book about tennis, and the San Francisco Fish Market. The same kind of intrusions undoubtedly entered your awareness as you tried to concentrate solely on the burning candle image.

If you could see a running list of all the random thoughts that occurred to you in the course of a day you would be amazed at the number and variety—and perhaps embarrassed by the trivia that fill your consciousness.

There is an old Indian saying that the mind is a drunken monkey. It stumbles and chatters and flits from one random thought to the next with little rhyme or reason. Even practiced meditators have difficulty focusing their complete attention on a single object or idea. They speak of rising to higher levels of meaning when they are finally able to direct their undivided attention for more than a minute.

When you hold a strong belief about something, that belief will naturally pop into your awareness when you find yourself in circumstances related to it. After years and years of practice, there is no way to suddenly stop this mental association from happening. Does this habitual association mean that you have no control over your thinking? Not at all. As you have seen, you can give yourself directions to produce images and feelings that you would not have experienced without those self-instructions. Does this mean you have anything approaching full control of the thoughts that occur to you? This can hardly be the case with a drunken monkey in charge.

A Case for Limited Control

What you do have is a limited ability to choose the *direction* of your thoughts and images, but only with a great many intrusions and random side tracks. Long held and practiced Psycho-Logic, learned at crucial times from influential sources, can hardly be expected to vanish with any single decision or shot of wishful thinking. You cannot choose to prevent maladaptive Psycho-Logic Evaluations or Tactics from entering your mind, but you can make decisions to prevent them from controlling you. You can also choose to multiply your options geometrically by deliberately selecting more adaptive Counter Logic perspectives—and by establishing Counter Tactics that realistically support whatever Counter Logic you select.

Aiming the Brain

If the Psycho-Logic you're working on originates on the emotional right side of the brain, why not work directly with the right side? There is now plenty of evidence—mostly from the emerging science of athletics—that you can directly control which side of the brain you want to operate.

Paul Pesthy, an Olympic Pentathlon champion (a grueling five-event competition), refocuses his right brain attention between events by placing a towel over his head, closing his eyes, and drawing a large circle in his imagination with the number "10" written just inside its boundary. He then draws an imaginary circle inside the first one, moves the 10 from the outside of the smaller circle to the inside, replaces that 10 with a "9," and continues with this very difficult mental sequence until he has internally constructed an imaginary target of ten perfect circles, numbered in descending order. In this way he feels he is targeting his right brain attention for the next event while distracting his left brain from telling him "what to do" and "how difficult it's going to be."

Tim Gallwey has developed several interesting methods for teaching tennis players to use the intuitive, nonverbal right brain. Many of his techniques have to do with focusing on right-brain images. For example, instead of rehashing, "Oh-oh, I missed the ball again," over and over in your mind, Gallwey suggests an image of tennis as an exercise in art appreciation.

"You just look at the court and net as a kind of three-dimensional canvas. Each new trajectory of the ball is then perceived as a new line on the drawing. The player sees the ball from an aesthetic point of view and regards its path as he would a line drawn by an artist. He notices not only the *shape* of the line, but the way it relates to others in the drawing, especially that of the net. To notice the relationship between the ball's trajectory and the net, and particularly to see the space between the two, demands great attention and therefore absorbs the mind. At the same time, this exercise forces sophisticated data about the clearance of the ball over the (net) lines....It also keeps the mind so absorbed in the reality of the ball that it forgets to doubt, try hard, condemn or over-instruct itself."

Other exercises involve seeing the ball as a moon following the natural laws of light and shadow as it moves from one side of the net to the other. Another involves imagining yourself as actually riding the ball as it gracefully moves back and forth, from one side to the other. Several baseball players have talked about improving their batting averages by "intently imagining" that they can "see" the stitching on the seams of the baseball as it hurls toward them from the pitcher's mound. Gallwey calls these exercises *forms of meditation* because they involve a means of *"focusing one's awareness fully on some object, idea, activity or state of being."*

Another Gallwey image invites the tennis player to consider each hit of the ball as a separate event—and to pay particular attention to the way each event approaches, strikes, and recedes into the past. Consider how most events in *life* occur in this way. As an event approaches, you increasingly anticipate it with whatever nervousness, delight, or Psycho-Logic you have learned to associate with that kind of event. The event strikes. You deal with its immediacy, for better or worse. It recedes into the past. You begin anticipating the next event, and on and on.

In Psycho-Logic terms, Gallwey's procedures fit this format...

"Inner Tennis" Psycho-Logic

S. — Survival Assumption (in this game).
   Hit the ball successfully.

E. — Evaluation.

I do better by concentrating on the ball than concentrating on myself.

T. — Tactics.

The ball is a moon.

Thin Think

One of the practical ways mental images are used to control everyday behavior is with the highly difficult and emotional problem of overeating. The best guesstimate is that there are between 40 and 80 million overweight Americans—or about one-quarter of the total population. Many of these unhappy eaters are on lifetime yo-yo diets that boost the sales of diet products in January and February, right after the traditional holiday eating spree, and again in May and June, just before time to squeeze into a bikini.

Psychologists have known for years that the problem is not the lack of knowledge about what to eat, but rather the actual self-control in eating habits. Psychologist John Horan and colleagues at Pennsylvania State University decided to apply an image technique to the problems of dieting.

Those in one group in their study were asked to pause a few seconds before putting anything in their mouths, close their eyes and attempt to develop a clear, vivid image of the fat slobs they could become if they continued their excessive eating. Those in a second group were asked to develop a positive image of how attractive and sexy they would be if they actually got their eating habits under control. Then both groups were allowed to eat whatever they chose.

While both groups lost weight over the eight-week study, only 35 percent of the subjects in the "think fat" group met the criterion of at least 1 pound off per week, while 75 percent of those in the "think thin" group were able to reach this goal. One of the subjects in the "think fat" group told the researchers, "Thinking about all those awful images made me depressed, so I found myself eating *more.*"

These results clearly suggest that *focusing on a positive image about what you are trying to accomplish,* just prior to engaging in the related eating behavior, can help you make decisions that get you beyond the immediate pleasures of that coconut cream pie on the refrigerator shelf. This kind of positive image is much better at getting through to the nonverbal right brain, because that's where the image is created. And, after all, it's the nonlogical, crazy right brain that thinks it can eat everything in sight and stay skinny at the same time. When the bikini image is in your awareness at the same instant as the coconut pie, at least a choice is possible. In this study, the skinny images were much more effective than the usual verbal advice. These women already knew the right words—and had repeated them over and over to themselves hundreds of times, but the new skinny image found a way of getting through to a control center where words don't count.

Batman and Robin

A right brain image often works when left brain words are ineffective. Psychologist Arnold Lazarus was working with an eight-year-old boy who knew it was "dumb" to be afraid of going to the dentist, but who felt afraid anyway. Instead of trying to "talk" him out of it (a typical left brain procedure), Lazarus decided to try a directed image approach.

"The sequence consisted of having the child picture himself accompanying Batman and Robin on various adventures and then imagining his heroes visiting the dentist while he observed them receiving dental attention. He was asked to picture this scene at least five times daily for one week. Next, he was to imagine himself in the dentist's chair while Batman and Robin stood by and observed. He also practiced this image several times a day for one week. He visited the dentist the following week and according to his mother he sat through four fillings without flinching."

Blowup

George Bernard Shaw once said, when he was an old man, "I've had a lot of fears in my life—most of which never happened." There is always a danger of creating expectations of catastrophe and then frightening ourselves with them *as if* they were reality. Arnold Lazarus has worked out a way of challenging these "scare yourself" expectations using a directed imagery technique called "blowup." Since you are already exaggerating what is only *possible*, Lazarus suggests that you exaggerate this possibility even further, until even you can see the absurdity of what you're doing. He gives an example of a man who had developed an irrational (right-brained) fear that the men's room in the movie theater might catch on fire at any minute. Since the man liked to go to the movies, he was left with a constant uneasy feeling that he had to go check out the men's room—or at least worry about checking it out—to see if it was on fire. This is an exaggerated case of the more ordinary kind of "checking" all of us do when we get a feeling that we forgot to lock the front door or left the electric blanket on. How many times have you gone back and found the door locked and blanket off?

Lazarus advised this man to create the following "movie image" in his head—"When the urge to check comes over you, do not leave your seat. Instead, I want you to imagine that fire has indeed broken out. First, picture the toilet paper and the toilet seats catching fire and spreading to the doors, then going along the floor, so that eventually the entire men's room is ablaze. Think as you sit in your seat, imagining the crackling flames spreading outside the men's room into the lobby, the carpets quickly catch fire and soon the entire movie house or theater is a roaring inferno. Still sitting in your seat, imagine the entire neighborhood on fire. Firemen battle the blaze unsuccessfully as all neighboring areas catch fire until the entire city is devoured. Still the flames keep spreading. One city after another is demolished in this voracious chain reaction until the entire country is ablaze. The flames even spread across the oceans until the entire world is on fire. Eventually the whole universe is one raging inferno."

When you've exaggerated the fear so far that it starts to seem amusing, you've got it.

Selecting an Image to Aim At

Images are commonly used to rehearse a role we admire. I can clearly remember walking out of a John Wayne movie when I was in junior high school, striding up and down the aisle at Read's Drug Store; ready to turn, draw and fire at the slightest hint of a gun slinger coming up behind me. I also remember sitting around that junior high school yard with my best buddy, Ken Schwarz, making up roles and images that might help us approach our number one problem—"How do you talk to a girl?" We even imagined what John Wayne might say.

I was reminded of that years later when I saw a client who used a model image to counter an unflattering image she had of herself. She had recently moved from another part of the state and transferred to a smaller branch of the state university, where she was enrolled in the middle of her sophomore year. It was a time in her life when she had lost a lot of weight, was getting more sophisticated in taking care of her appearance, and wanted to lose her old image as a "fat, dumpy, middle child, who never had anything intelligent to say."

We talked about this, and I asked her if there was anyone she admired who seemed to exhibit what she was trying to accomplish for herself. The name and the role that came to her mind was Faye Dunaway, whom she had just seen as a flawless, sophisticated lady in "The Thomas Crown Affair" with Steve McQueen. I suggested that when my client wasn't sure how to handle herself, she ask herself how Faye Dunaway might handle things. I was hoping that this counter image might suggest alternative Tactics and might also model a style of handling things that would counter her poor self-Evaluation.

A week or so later, she told me how it was going. "Funny," she said, "I walk across campus as if I own the place. I feel different—as if some of those other people want to change places with *me*. Imagine that—change places with *me*. And here I am, pretending to be someone else."

She never did turn out to be Faye Dunaway, but a couple of years later she's a long way from where she started, and a lot happier with where she is now.

Using Images

A Counter Logic image can be used in the same way as a Counter Logic phrase...

1. Think of a positive image that counters the Psycho-Logic you are trying to change (imagine, for example, the attention you'll get in your bikini when you lose twenty pounds).
2. Practice this image for a few minutes until you vividly experience the good feelings that go with it.

3. Deliberately use this image as an alternative to particular Tactics (such as overeating) or Evaluations (I'm too fat).

The Buddha Businessman

A fifty-three-year-old business manager decided to use a Counter Image to control his peptic ulcer. His doctor had told him to calm down and learn how to take it easy, or he would have to quit his job and start spending some time in the hospital.

"Peptic Ulcer" Psycho-Logic

S. — Survival Assumption.

It's essential to be a business success (in order to maintain the family status and my own status as a "useful" person).

E. — Evaluation.

I have to keep abreast of every business detail and make all the right decisions or risk letting my status slip away.

T. — Tactic.

Maintain a high state of alertness and constant vigil (i.e. a high state of tension).

This was a bright man who had done a lot of reading about Far Eastern religions. He decided to base his Counter Logic on an image of peace and calm he had read about.

"Inner Peace" Counter Logic

Counter Image	I "see" myself sitting on a cliff high above a raging sea—a fierce storm approaching, its wind already swirling furiously around my body. But I am protected—surrounded by a glowing energy field of light and warmth that keeps all traces of the storm from touching me. I am in relaxed control of myself—in an alert state of meditation— aware of the storm around me but perfectly calm in its presence.
Counter Tactics	At business meetings, or at other times of tension—focus on this image to calm myself down—to allow all tension to

flow from my body—to remind me that I can control my inner state of calmness, no matter what the turmoil around me.

After using his calmness program for several weeks he found himself making better decisions than ever. He was able to think more clearly. He was relying more on inner control and less on a bottle of Maalox.

Image Sources

Images that naturally occur to you are often the best since they are totally your own creation. The Sugar Bird Lady who saw herself as a bird eating sugar from her husband's hand might use this naturally occuring image to generate more tender feelings toward her husband. I could use my John Wayne image to help me confront a difficult or hostile colleague.

Other Counter Images...

• Walking across campus with an image of Faye Dunaway to help you generate or regain a lost sense of confidence.
• Walking down the "road of life"—or down the Yellow Brick Road—as a reminder to live in the present instead of waiting until you reach some final destination.
• Focusing on a memory of accomplishment or pride to remind you that such things did happen to you.
• Developing a positive future image of yourself—your own body in a summertime bikini—to encourage you toward an important Counter Logic goal.
• Using an image of someone important to you or someone you admire to guide or advise you. (What would that person do in a situation like this, or what would he or she advise you to do?)
• Visualizing yourself scaling the face of a treacherous mountain—or performing some other difficult feat—as an analogy for a difficult Psycho-Logic change.
• Totally exaggerating a fear or worry as a way of putting your anxiety in perspective (instead of imagining your dinner hostess merely rejecting you, actually visualize her dumping a plate of spaghetti on your head).

- Imagine yourself actually beating up or stomping that person you hate—the one who always intimidates you—as a way of draining some of your hostile energy. You may find it easier to deal with him or her next time.

- Turning around a memory that helped you uncover Psycho-Logic. If you remember "never" catching the ball, search your memory banks for that *one time* when you did. Focus on the good feeling that came when the ball was in your hand, and consider the Tactics of learning how to catch a ball—or whatever else—that might generate those feelings again.

- If your Psycho-Logic leaves you dwelling on the past, focus on a positive and possible image of your future—one that thinking about helps you work toward.

- Construct an image (like Sugar Bird Lady's) that reminds you of something positive in a relationship that you care about—an image that might help you move that relationship to a more meaningful or satisfying level.

Images can be begged, borrowed, or stolen just like Counter Logic phrases. Television—especially commercials—can be a good resource. The "life-and-a-cola" image might lead you to Tactics of creating more joyful moments in your own life. An image of "reaching out and touching someone" can remind you to reach out in person as well as over the telephone. The Counter Logic Shopping List may suggest images that are more powerful than these Counter Logic phrases.

Images or Words

The kind of image you are looking for is one that leads your emotions away from Psycho-Logic you are trying to change and in the direction of your new Counter Logic. You should always consider whether a counter image or Counter Logic phrase would have the greatest emotional impact. You might even consider using both, alternating your strategy between the two. Whichever you use, a written list of Counter Tactics should be developed to go along with it.

Counter Logic

Counter Logic	An emotional image or phrase to challenge an old Evaluation or Survival Assumption.
Counter Tactics	A specific list of methods for making your new Counter Logic a functional part of your everyday life.

12

Keeping What
You Get

Selecting another way to look at a situation is the first and simplest step in Psycho-Logic self-regulation. Advice of this kind is a dime a dozen—it's all over the place—and some of it isn't bad. "Do unto others as you would have them do unto you" is beautiful Counter Logic that can help you out of your isolation and involve you in "doing" for others. The *Bible* provides many other examples. So do the *Koran* and the *The Prophet*. So does Norman Vincent Peale's *The Power of Positive Thinking* and Dale Carnegie's *How to Win Friends and Influence People*. You can find terrific Counter Logic on cereal box tops, TV commercials, old Beatle albums, and John Wayne reruns. There is certainly no lack of good advice—or catchy ways of putting it.

My own Counter Logic shopping list is probably no better or worse than most. As you looked through it, you probably found a couple of good ideas, as well as some silly ones. That's because it's *my* shopping list. Yours would obviously be based on your needs, and even mine is locked within a narrow time frame. Next week's shopping list will always be a little different.

Fifty-Fifty

Wayne Dyer gives an example of useful Counter Logic in his book, *Your Erroneous Zones*.

> You know that at least half of the people in your world are going to disagree with at least half the things you say. If this is accurate (and you need only look at 'landslide' elections to see

that forty-four percent of the population voted against the winner), then you will always have about a fifty-fifty chance of getting some disapproval whenever you express an opinion.

Armed with this knowledge, you can begin to look at disapproval in a new light. When someone disapproves of something you say, instead of being hurt, or instantly shifting your opinion to gain praise, you can remind yourself that you've just run into one of those folks in the fifty percent who don't agree with you ... Once you expect it, you won't be inclined to hurt yourself with it.

Once you expect *what?* Simply reality. There will always be someone who disagrees with you, whether you expect that to happen or not. By accepting that reality, and by using Dyer's Counter Logic to deal with it, you avoid discouraging yourself when the inevitable happens. (Notice that *you* are the one inflicting the discouragement, and not the person doing the discouraging.)

Dyer's good advice is something that strikes you as sensible when you read it, but which you often forget ten minutes after you put the book back on the shelf. The advice is good because it represents a positive way of dealing with disapproval that *could* help you handle it more effectively. *How do you get it off the page of Dyer's book and into your awareness when you need it?* Dyer explains the reality, and he gives you the Counter Logic to deal with it, but the training and practice that might enable you to use it are up to you. Getting it out of the book and into *your head* does not take a great deal of effort, but it does take more than reading about it. Ordinarily it takes (1) some way of remembering it, (2) some systematic practice for a day or so before you actually apply it (but only for twenty-second periods of focused concentration, spaced throughout the day), followed by (3) a deliberate application of a Counter Logic phrase like, "That's the *other* fifty percent!" in a real situation where someone disapproves of you.

It's easy to see the difference between this kind of systematic approach to changing Psycho-Logic, and skimming over a piece of good advice one time in a three-hundred-page book.

Instant Change

Sometimes you do run across Counter Logic that makes an instant difference the moment you hear it—without any practice. I remember once seeing the parents of a mentally retarded girl who never knew what to expect from their daughter, and were never quite sure how to handle her. I talked to them about I.Q. numbers, but that didn't do much good, so I was surprised when they came back the following week and told me that things were going "a 100 percent better!" What had happened? They had seen their family physician in the meantime and were telling him about the results of my testing when he happened to comment that "her mind was more like that of a ten-year-old than that of someone her real age—fifteen." That turned out to be an extremely useful way for these parents to think about their daughter's limitations—and abilities. It was a *good map of reality that showed them what to expect,* and gave them more understanding about how to handle a ten-year-old girl in a fifteen-year-old body. The parents found themselves in a much better frame of mind to help their daughter work toward her real potential, instead of constantly arguing about what that potential was. When you ask the parents how they were able to accomplish this, they tell you, "We just think of her as ten, but still learning."

Spending Big

A psychologist I know once told me of his ambition to become financially independent by buying and operating a string of rental properties. Terrific idea, but he had been making good money for five years and never managed to save any of it until the last six months. Now he smiles when he tells me that he is "finally on his way." Why the switch? His early memories about money mostly involve not having any. That's what started his dream of financial independence in the first place. He remembers one specific Saturday afternoon when his father asked *him* for a three dollar "loan." All he had was the five dollars he had earned delivering groceries at the local A & P. That childhood loan to his father turned out to be an unreturned gift. As an adult, he always felt empty with less than fifty dollars in his pocket and would find himself getting angry when he wasn't able to buy little things whenever a whim struck him. He seemed to be constantly caught between his spend-right-now Tactics and his Evaluation that he would never be satisfied without financial independence. There just didn't seem to be any way to spend it all and save it up at the same time. There was a price to pay no matter which way he went.

Then came a Counter Logic switch. He was walking through a boat show, looking at some of the $100,000 cruisers, when it suddenly occurred to him what a small-time spender he was. All he had was six pairs of sunglasses and a *Playboy* magazine. It struck him that the *idea* of SPENDING BIG—if he could keep it in mind—might be enough to motivate him actually to work in that direction. The Counter Logic idea of "Spending Big" is what finally got him to start an automatic payroll account and curtail when he now saw as penny ante spending. He was on his way.

Now You've Got It—Now You Don't

Some good ideas have an instant impact, but one that doesn't last very long. Almost anything is likely to occur to the drunken monkey of your mind at one time or another. You are bound to come up with good Counter Logic once in a while—and sometimes even take it seriously enough to think, "Next time I'm gonna do this thing differently," but when next time comes you've already forgotten your good intentions, and end up riding the same old merry-go-round—right back to where you started. You've finally gotten something together, only to catch yourself back in the same old pattern an hour or day later...

You were determined to quit smoking this time, but when you looked down you noticed another cigarette in your hand.

Norman Vincent Peale tells you to think positive and "do it genuinely," so you go out and *think positive* for the next ten minutes, but by lunch you catch yourself thinking negative again.

Dale Carnegie says the sweetest sound in any language is a person's own name, so you go around George-ing and Phyllis and Henry and Frank-ing everybody, until it occurs to you on the third day that you forgot to first-name anybody all morning. You think it wasn't a bad idea, and maybe you'll start it up again sometime, but you drop it for right now.

You look in the mirror one morning and really plan to stick to your diet this time, but by dinner you've already decided to make up for an extra piece of chocolate cake by trying to cut down even further the next day.

Why do most good advice and good intentions have such a transitory impact? For one thing, when you become aware of a useful perspective (Evaluation) or way of doing something (Tactics), your concentration is focused on *that thought* or idea for *that moment*, and not on your ordinary way of thinking. When you are inspired by the exploits of James Bond or Faye Dunaway, you may walk out of the theater in a Bond-Dunaway frame of mind but by the time you get to the drug store and remember to pick up some toothpaste and soda water, the Bond-Dunaway effect has already vanished behind the distractions of mundane reality.

It's not surprising that Counter Logic one-liners and cute sayings—no matter how true they may be—have little effect against years of practicing contradictory Psycho-Logic. It's common to hear people say, "I try to look at things differently, but it just isn't *me.*" Deep down, we're all that person we've come to believe in so much that any major change seems like personal treason. Most programs of attitude change tell us how we "ought to think," but give us little practical advice on how to push it through the resistance of our own thick skulls. Old ways of reacting die hard—especially when they serve an important emotional function. Lifelong Psycho-Logic can hardly be expected to vanish at the flash to sudden insight. It is much more likely that the *insight* will vanish—and, in fact, that's often what happens.

An insight has to be rediscovered and reinterpreted many times before it begins to have any impact on the Psycho-Logic reality of someone's life. It would be nice if initial understanding—that "ah-ha" experience—suddenly changed everything and made you fresh and beautiful, but it doesn't often work that way. Understanding must always be followed by painstaking implementation until the new awareness begins to have a life of its own. The therapist's repetition was clearly an essential element in treating the "Yellow Ribbon" lady who lost her son. By using the Counter Logic "Let him go! Let him go!" the therapist forced this mother to confront the death of her son again and again, while her Psycho-Logic was trying to keep him alive. It was good Counter Logic, combined with repetition, that finally won the struggle.

A married nursing student, who derived Tactics from her Evaluation, "People won't like me if I tell them how I *really* feel," was finally able to tell her husband how she wanted him to treat her sexually, but was still unable to tell the cafeteria lady that she liked her hamburger without mayonnaise. She said it made her feel "pushy." She got the insight in her head, but was only getting it in her life one slice at a time.

The "insight" part of psychotherapy is really fairly easy. A good therapist is usually aware of at least one or two Survival Assumptions within the first couple of sessions. Pointing these out to the client, or helping him discover them for himself, is not usually that difficult either. The real accomplishment of psychotherapy—when it's successful—is discovering over and over again how you are continually doing the same thing in one disguise after the other. Eventually the client has heard it and seen it so much, and in so many connections, that he no longer has the option of fooling himself. The therapist has brought his attention back to it so often that, even when it is disguised, it is still recognized for what it is. At first, the client begins to recognize it only *after* he does it, then he catches himself right in the middle of doing it and, finally, he can see the Psycho-Logic coming up. He can see himself being tempted. Only then is he free to disconnect himself from it and stick in something else.

Once Is Never Enough

Awareness, by itself, does not create instant change—it merely provides a renewed potential for it. The importance of understanding your Psycho-Logic is in the fact that you are no longer *blindly* compelled to follow it. Even if a Counter Logic alternative can be found, a decision to follow it must be made and remade over and over again.

One of the real signs of progress in therapy is when a person catches herself in the middle of some Psycho-Logic she has decided to change. That's progress because choice is only possible when it's available at a choice point. You have to catch yourself doing something before you can change how you are doing it.

Like most old soldiers, battle-hardened Psycho-Logic doesn't die with every challenge—but it does tend to weaken when a Counter Logic contender gains strength through repeated confrontation. You have only limited control over habitual Psycho-Logic, but the more new Counter Logic is applied against old Psycho-Logic, the more the

Counter Logic gets established as the automatic habit pattern. The less it is applied—especially in the beginning—the more the old Psycho-Logic tends to nip it in the bud.

Catching Yourself

Psycho-Logic affects you automatically. For Counter Logic to have an effect, it must be applied deliberately. The more you practice Counter Logic, the more it will be on your mind and the more you will be aware of opportunities to apply it. If you suffer from Psycho-Logic anxiety, practicing a relaxing Counter Logic alternative will automatically connect your anxiety with your new Counter Logic. When you catch yourself in an anxious situation your Counter Logic will be in place and ready to use. Having a practiced alternative gives you the power to control your anxiety—and the direction of your life—one situation at a time.

Hundred-Trial Learning

When it comes to implementing Counter Logic, "one-trial learning" is rare. You didn't learn that you are shy, or jealous, or courageous or worry a lot because you did these things one time, but because you found yourself doing them, or being told about them, over and over again. Psychotherapy gives you a chance to counteract this repeated learning by encouraging you to *repeatedly* reflect on what it is you are doing. Eventually, you no longer need that help because you are able to see it for yourself.

The missing ingredient from most self-change programs is the element of repetition and ritualistic involvement for a period long enough to make a difference. It's easy enough to uncover an ineffective Psycho-Logic SET, and even easier to develop new Counter Logic that might be more productive. It is considerably more difficult to repeatedly substitute an *intellectual,* left-brain truth that contradicts an emotional, right-brain "truth" you learned to survive on.

In any relearning process, old habits maintain partial control while new ones are being learned. The new habits frequently feel awkward and mechanical in the beginning. Riding a bike or roller skating felt stilted and a little frightening until the lateral balance and movement of the wheels became a natural part of your own balance system. New Counter Logic only begins to have *emotional* meaning when enough practice has given it a chance to fit into the natural flow of your life. In the meantime, you can concentrate on building up its habit strength by finding opportunities to practice. If the Counter Logic you select has inherent emotional meaning *for you,* what at first feels mechanical will gradually become a natural part of your new understanding.

The temptation to engage in old Psycho-Logic will especially reoccur when you find yourself in situations similar to those in which you learned it. This is why some people never learn to deal with their parents on anything but a childish level. It is also true—as you have already demonstrated with your mind focus exercise—that you can deliberately control the focus of your attention to an alternative Counter Logic phrase or image whenever you choose to do so. The problem is remembering to refocus when the new Counter Logic is of value—and having the Counter Logic ready the instant you need it.

Given all the forces working against Psycho-Logic change, it is amazing how easily a change can be accomplished. A key element is in a small amount of *prior* practice, so that (1) the *new* Counter Logic is already attached to situations *before* they occur and, (2) the new Counter Logic has acquired at least some of the same habit power that keeps the old Psycho-Logic alive.

With as little as ten minutes of practice, spaced out over ten one-minute intervals during the course of a single day, you will already be able to experience a significant sense of power to challenge maladaptive Psycho-Logic that has been in place for twenty years or more. There is no magic and there are no shortcuts here. Ten minutes, ten times, means ten minutes, ten times. Once or twice for one or two minutes just won't do the job. That's why you are so often disappointed when you get a good idea, and say to yourself, "I've got to remember this one," but end up forgetting it as quickly as it came. One trial learning doesn't work here, so there is no use setting yourself up for disappointement by expecting it. What actually is required works quickly enough, but less than that isn't worth doing.

Day Tripping

The easiest way to get a feel for the amount of subjective control you can actually have is by putting it to a one-day test. Although a one-day exercise will obviously not be enough to turn your life around, it will be enough to show you that a difference *can* be made. It will also give you a working experience with internal self-control that you can apply in a number of useful ways. If you are willing to give it a try, here are the steps involved...

Select a Counter Logic phrase or image. Look for one that immediately strikes you as potentially useful. Then put it into a short, positively worded phrase or a simple but powerful image that could represent a higher or more constructive level of understanding *for you.* Chose one that contradicts a Psycho-Logic SET you are trying to change. You can steal Counter Logic from my list or someone else's, or you can create it yourself, but you may have to reword it to give its meaning your own personal touch. If you do steal one, it is not necessary for you to agree with the original author's definition, or even to know what it is, nor is it necessary for you to fully understand the meaning yourself, since your experience using it will generate a meaning of its own.

Memorize it word for word, or focus on the image until you instantly "see it" the moment you try. This should be fairly easy, since it should be no longer than a short sentence or more complex than a simple image. Any wording or image more complicated than this needs to be condensed to get to the heart of the matter.

Set up a reminder system. This step is crucial, since this is what is usually left out of most self-change systems—and a major reason why many of them fail. A reminder system should be something simple and unobtrusive, but strategically placed so that you cannot fail to notice it in your daily routine. I often use something like a question mark, or a small red dot, printed on a half-inch piece of cardboard, scotch-taped to the telephone or in the middle of the car speedometer. Some clients of mine have used a plain unobtrusive piece of scotch tape over the faces of their watches. A reminder, in the form of a small picture or word, can also be taped to the refrigerator door or placed on a desk or a table that you frequently use. If you smoke, an "X" on the top or side of your cigarette carton is a reminder you can't help but notice many times throughout the day. The simpler the reminder is, the better. It should contain very little meaning in itself and need not contain the actual Counter Logic you are working on. Experience has shown that Counter Logic is often learned more quickly when the learner is required to regenerate it, rather than simply reread it. Ultimately, you are working toward a spontaneous ability to generate the new Counter Logic when a real situation or an old piece of Psycho-Logic acts as a cue.

An important thing to keep in mind about reminder systems is that they work only for a short time. After several days, they start to blend in with the furniture like anything else that loses its initial "startle impact." This loss of effect is ordinarily no problem, since you need a reminder only in the beginning. Still, you may find it necessary to change your reminder system once or twice, or reposition it, so that it has the kind of renewed impact that will attract your attention again.

Initially repeat the Counter Logic phrase or focus on the Counter-Logic image at least six times during the first day. Your reminder system will automatically cue you to do this. Each repetition time should last about twenty seconds, but no more than a minute, and each should be spaced at least an hour apart. Short, consistent practice periods are much more effective than one or two long ones.

On each occasion, you should *focus your full attention* on the words or on the image, but otherwise allow your mind and body to relax as much as possible. By the third or fourth practice session, the Counter Logic will begin to associate itself automatically with physical relaxation. They will flow together more easily—each helping and reinforcing the other.

During these twenty-second to one-minute practice periods, you should continue silently repeating or visualizing the new Counter Logic, deliberately and with emphasis. There should be no attempt to figure out any new meaning, although you should make a mental note of new feelings or new thoughts that occur to you. New insights will spontaneously emerge if the Counter Logic you selected strikes a harmonious emotional chord. When the twenty seconds or the minute is up, go back to your normal routine, but feel free to take along any new insight or feeling that naturally overlaps.

Evaluate and reenergize new meanings. Toward the end of the day, spend the last one-minute session refocusing on your new Counter Logic, while allowing all the meaning and feeling that occurred to you during that day to reoccur to you again—along with any new insight that comes to you now. With the total of this new awareness in your mind, take a moment to evaluate the overall effect that this Counter Logic has had on you, and to judge whether it was worth ten minutes of your time and concentration.

The requirements for getting Counter Logic in your life are fairly simple then—select and memorize or visualize potentially useful Counter Logic; devise a reminder system to insure that you will remember to use what you selected; run through the Counter Logic six separate times during the day, giving it your full attention for at least twenty seconds while associating it with physical relaxation; and, finally, reevaluate and reinforce any positive lessons you learned.

Putting It into Practice

You may have noticed that Tactics have not been mentioned in terms of practice—only Counter Logic phrases or images. This is because it is easier to start from the inside out. *External change flows much more easily when it follows an internal change.* You should always spend at least a day—and perhaps several—practicing a Counter Logic phrase or image before you attempt any change in external Tactics. You should already be catching yourself in Psycho-Logic situations where Counter Tactics *could* be applied before you actually try to apply any. When you are finally ready to put your new Tactics into practice, the Tactics will easily fit right into place.

Suppose you are operating from a "shyness Psycho-Logic" that you are trying to change. You've already figured out your Psycho-Logic SET...

"Shyness" Psycho-Logic

S. — Survival Assumption.

It's essential to be liked (need for attention and approval).

E. — Evaluation.

I'm such a "middle-of-the-road *nothing*" that no one ever pays attention to me.

T. — Tactic.

Blend into the background of relationships, social events, and family affairs.

You have selected an alternative Counter Logic...

"Getting Involved" Counter Logic

Counter Image	Peel the Onion (from the Shopping List—this is an image that suggests getting beyond the superficiality of relationships by peeling away the layers toward a person's inner core).
Counter Tactics	1. Start remembering people's names, instead of being so nervous you never really hear them. When you meet someone again, use his or her name and say something pleasant—even just "hello."
	2. Start asking people about themselves. Ask them what their day was like. Find out what they think is important or what they like to do. Check out their opinions. Find out what they are good at that they could teach you about or show you.
	3. Jot down interesting ideas, thoughts or news items—along with the name of someone who might like to hear about that. Slide it into the conversation the next time you're at a loss for what to say.
	4. When you're at a party or social gathering, approach someone with a smile and a conversational lead ("I'm Jody's neighbor" or "Hello, I'm _____ I'm not sure where to hang my coat.")

For the first couple of days, you practice your "Onion Peeling" image. You draw a little onion on a file card and set it on your desk as a reminder to practice. Then take it home and put it on your dresser. Three or four times in the morning and a couple of times in the afternoon you spend a minute focusing on this image—in a way that reminds you of a brief meditation or self-hypnosis. You don't apply any new Tactics but having this Counter Logic in your mind helps you notice times when you could.

After the third day of practice you decide to start *doing* things differently, using some of your new Tactics. The first few times are a little awkward but the mental habit you've built up keeps you going until things begin to smooth out. After a couple of weeks of using your attention-paying Tactics, even you can't help notice that people are starting to pay more attention to you. You'll never be the star of the office—and don't want to be—but if things keep going the way they have been, you'll be more than satisfied with the results of your efforts.

Counter Logic Combat Cards

A Counter Logic combat card is a 3 × 5 file card with the Psycho-Logic you want to combat written on one side and the Counter Logic you are combating it with written on the other. Carol's combat card looked like this...

Side A

"Fear of Intimacy" Psycho-Logic

S — It's essential to be loved and cared for.
E — I used to be loved but I lost it (first when my mother went to work, then when my sister deserted me and—the final straw—when Daddy wanted me to be a boy).
T — Don't get close to people (or you'll risk losing or disappointing them too).

Side B

"Self Disclosure" Counter Logic

Counter Logic

• Mother didn't desert me—she just had to go to work.
• Joan didn't desert me—she just grew up.
• Dad really *did* want me to be a boy. So who's problem is that!?
• I lose the thing I want for fear of losing it.
• No one gets loved *all* the time, but maybe I could get some of it some of the time.

Counter Tactic (for beginning to get involved)
    Be more superficially friendly.

It is only through repeatedly challenging old Psycho-Logic that a significant and lasting change is possible. A combat card represents your commitment to the challenge and your personal plan for carrying it out.

You can carry a combat card in your pocket or purse as a reminder to practice your Counter Logic throughout the day. Each time you notice the card, you should focus your full attention on one item. The first time you might challenge your irrational Psycho-Logic Evaluation; the next time you might choose to concentrate on the implications of a single Counter Logic Tactic and so on. When you catch yourself engaged in the old Psycho-Logic a quick glance at the Psycho-Logic side of your combat card will instantly show you the arbitrariness of what you are doing. Flipping over to the Counter Logic side will give you an alternative immediately. By putting a small mark beside each point you review, or beside a Tactic you actually use, you have an ongoing report card of your progress.

A combat card should be flexible. You can set it up in whatever way best suits your purpose. One young man wrote "I'm not good enough!" as his Psycho-Logic Evaluation. On the other side, he wrote for his Counter Logic, "I'm not good enough *for Dad!*" Instead of constantly repeating to himself, "I'm not good enough," he began practicing and substituting, "I'm not good enough *for Dad.*" These last two words made all the difference in the world in his effort to look at himself more realistically.

Personal Worth

A social worker decided to use a combat card to solve a personal conflict over raising her rates...

Side A

"Price War" Psycho-Logic

S — It's important to be liked by all my clients and respected by all my colleagues (need for approval).

E — If I raise my rates my clients won't like me (I'll lose business). If I don't increase my rates up to the local standard my colleagues won't like me (I'll lose friends).

T — Keep my rates the same, but fret about them all the time.

Side B

"Self-Worth" Counter Logic

Counter Logic (for settling my internal conflict)

Emotional Premise—I'm *not worth* $35 an hour.
Counter Arguments—
1. TV newscasters aren't worth $800 an hour.
2. In a market place I'm worth what a client is willing to pay.
3. I get paid for the time I spent in college, not just the hour I spend with a client.
4. If someone can't afford $35 I can always charge that person less.

5. If I help someone with depression or anxiety, it's worth far
more than $35. People usually thank me while they're writing
out a check.

Tactics

Raise my rates from $30 to $35.

She was a little surprised when none of her clients complained
about her rate hike. It made her more aware than ever that her
dilemma had more to do with her sense of personal worth than her
economic value.

Taking Charge Now

After you use a combat card for several days you may find that
you don't need it any longer. You will have conditioned yourself to
recognize those situations in which a Counter Logic choice is
possible. By being aware of your Psycho-Logic on a moment-by-
moment basis, you give yourself a continuing choice, and it's through
that choice that your life belongs to you.

13

Guilt:
Breaking Your Own Rules

You feel guilty for one of two reasons—you either do something you have a rule against doing, or you *don't* do something your rule says you "should" do.

"Guilt" Psycho-Logic

S. — Survival Assumption.

It's important (for survival of a good self-judgment) to think, behave, or feel a certain way.

E. — Evaluation.

I didn't do it but *I should have.*

T. — Tactic.

Mental (intellectual) and emotional self-punishment.

"Shoulding" on Yourself

A "should" may involve a conflict about something you'd like to do but think is "bad" or "bad for you." You want to do it but you don't want to feel guilty about it. Johnny masturbates but knows he shouldn't. He's sure that God and his mother would disapprove. He feels good while he's doing it, but he wallows in guilt when it's over.

Sometimes a "should" involves a conflict between two Survival Assumptions—perhaps between motherhood and career. Liv Ullman accepts an on-location movie role that takes her away from her daughter for months. She gets good reviews from the critics but her own judgment leaves her feeling guilty.

A "should" may involve a Survival Assumption that something is supposed to be perfect and an Evaluation that you "should" feel guilty if it isn't...

- A businesswoman has *The Washington Post* delivered every morning but rarely has time to read it. She feels guilty because intelligent people *should* read the newspaper.

- Brenda Harding is a working mother who cooks, cleans, does the laundry, writes letters to the kids in college, and pays the bills. When her husband asks why they ran out of his breakfast cereal she feels guilty for "falling behind."

- Among children who have attempted suicide, it is common to find that they feel guilty because they *should not* have masturbated or *should not* have wished someone were dead.

Where the Shoulds Come From

Psychologist Alberta Siegel says that "shoulds" are part of what keeps society from falling apart. When it comes to raising children, she says, "Every society is only twenty years away from barbarism. Twenty years is all we have to accomplish the task of civilizing the infants who are born into our midst each year.

"These savages know nothing of our language, our culture, our religion, our values, our customs of interpersonal relations.

"The infant is totally ignorant about communism, fascism, democracy, civil liberties, the rights of the minority as opposed to the prerogatives of the majority, respect, decency, honesty, customs, conventions, and manners.

"The barbarian must be tamed if civilization is to survive."

The job of mothers and fathers is to tame their little barbarians—to teach them when to feel guilty. I once watched a father teaching this to his five-year-old daughter at a roller rink. For some reason the daughter didn't like the looks of one of the other girls and gave her a shove that knocked her over on her skates. The father angrily told his daughter, "Hey, you hurt that little girl! What if I knocked you down like that. How would it make *you* feel? Now you just sit there until you're ready to apologize to that little girl!" This father was giving his daughter a lesson in why she "shouldn't" do such things.

A Traveler's Guide to Guilt Trips

There are several well-traveled roads that lead to guilt.

- Perfectionist standards (not being perfect)
- Not living up to expectations (yours or someone else's)
- Feeling tempted (guilt by association)
- Hostile feelings (toward children, wife, parents, etc.)
- Saying things you don't believe (lying)
- The new feminism (as it affects both men and women)
- Feeling guilty about feeling guilty (or for *not* feeling guilty)

Perfectionist Standards

People often feel guilty for failing—failing at marriage, failing at work, failing at life, but failure is always measured against some personal standard. If you swear to yourself you'll never smoke another cigarette, you feel guilty if you fall below your standard. If you expect to be a business tycoon by forty you start feeling like a guilty failure if you're still in middle management at thirty-eight.

Evelyn Stevens is one of those people who sets impossible standards ninety percent of the time. She feels guilty about almost everything—especially about not being married. ("I *should* be married by thirty.") She spends lots of time looking and comparing, but has very few second dates. She never seems to meet her "perfect match."

When Evelyn was growing up it was hard to tell that a little girl lived in her house. She was always made to clean her room before she left for school, and it was always checked to see that it was done "thoroughly." She was also expected to clean up her plate ("Every last bean, Young Lady!") and roll the toothpaste tube from the bottom. ("There's no sense wasting any.") Her mother even made her keep an extra pair of galoshes at school. "You never know when it might rain," her mother told her, "Sunny days can fool you." Little by little, the message sank in.

Evelyn's "Perfection" Psycho-Logic

S. — Survival Assumption.

It's important to *be perfect* and *do everything perfectly.*

E. — Evaluation.

I never seem to be quite perfect, no matter how hard I try.

T. — Tactic.

Keep striving harder and harder, while feeling guilty about every little imperfection along the way.

Not Living Up to Expectations

Even realistic expectations don't *always* work out. If you're used to working all your life, it's easy to slip into guilt when you suddenly lose your job. ("I *should* provide a pay check for my family," "I *should* have gotten more education," etc.) When your self-Evaluation is closely tied to your work, or to your financial contribution to your family, the loss of employment is as much a personal blow as a financial one.

Many of the jobless hold themselves personally responsible for their situation. Sociologist M. Harvey Brenner of Johns Hopkins University has found that a 1 percent increase of unemployment leads to a 4.1 percent increase in the suicide rate and a 3.4 percent increase in mental hospital admissions.

The Terrible Toos

Martha is a mother who constantly frets. She wonders if she gives her children enough of her time, if she's *too busy* to really listen to them—*too busy* to spend enough time with them. She feels guilty for wasting *too much* of her time on her writing and wonders if she's *too illiterate* to ever get anything published.

Thinking of yourself as *too* this or *too* that is a frequent road to the realm of guilt. You can feel guilty because you're...

- Too skinny, fat, bald, flat-chested, short-nosed, etc. (You feel guilty for not looking the way you "should.")

- Too ugly (You feel guilty for not being as beautiful as so-and-so.)

- Too attractive (Guilty feelings for having more than anyone else.)
- Too average (You "should" be better than average.)
- Too stupid (Guilty for not being smarter.)
- Too intelligent (Guilty for not living up to your potential.)
- Too famous (Guilty for getting too much attention.)
- Too unfamous (Guilty for not getting enough attention.)
- Too shy (Guilty for not being more assertive.)
- Too assertive (Guilty for hurting other people's feelings.)
- Too rigid (Guilty for not being flexible enough to compromise with loved ones.)
- Too flexible (Guilty for not standing up for yourself.)
- Too rich (You feel guilty for not earning it, or for not using it well.)
- Too poor (You "should" have been able to earn more.)
- Too hard-working (Guilty for not having more fun.)
- Too fun-loving (Guilty for not accomplishing enough.)
- Too upset or angry (Guilty for not controlling yourself.)
- Too objective (Guilty for not "feeling" enough.)
- Too sensitive (You feel guilty about *everything*—including your over-sensitivity.)
- Too insensitive (So why are you so sensitive about that?)
- Too idealistic (Guilty for never coming down to earth and getting involved in real life.)
- Too realistic (Guilty for never pursuing a dream.)
- Too success-oriented (Guilty for not knowing what's *really* important.)
- Too failure-oriented (Guilty for never succeeding.)
- Too dependent (Guilty for not standing on your own two feet.)
- Too independent (Guilty for never needing anyone.)
- Too cheerful and optimistic (Guilty of never feeling anything deeply.)
- Too chronically depressed (Guilty of missing the joy in life.)
- Too unhappy (Guilty of not being happier.)

Feeling Tempted

To be human is to have an active imagination. That means you are likely to think of anything and everything at one time or another—*especially those things that are tempting*. Just being tempted—without acting on it—often makes a person feel guilty. One study of grade school students showed that those who were tempted to cheat felt *more* guilty than those who actually cheated.

Hostile Feelings

It's easy enough to feel guilty for hating your husband or children. The rule says you're supposed to love them. Actually, it's normal to hate the ones you love once in awhile—or at least hate some of the things they do. The people you care about are exactly the ones who get under your skin. You don't hate what you don't care about—you feel indifferent.

There are times when it's hard to live with yourself. Living with someone else is bound to rub you raw some of the time.

Saying Things You Don't Believe

Children are sometimes asked to incriminate themselves. ("Tell me the truth about the awful thing you did and I *promise* not to punish you.") A lot of children don't trust adults enough to go that far out on a limb. They prefer to lie rather than turn themselves over to the mercy of the court—even though their lying compounds the guilt.

Everybody lies—at least in the sense of holding back on the total truth. If a friend goes to a lot of trouble to cook you a dinner that tastes bad, and then asks you how you liked it, you might be tempted to lie—or at least hedge your answer. If your boss asks how enthusiastic you are about his new project, you might fake a little more enthusiasm than you actually feel.

There's nothing wrong with an occasional compromise to protect someone's feelings—or to protect your job. It's when you apply too much sugar coating—when you compromise too much or too often—that guilty feelings start to stir. There are times when an issue is so important you either stand up for yourself or you suffer the guilt of bending over too far.

The New Feminism

Women try to be assertive and independent without giving up their vulnerability and feminine appeal. Men shoot for macho sexuality while developing their sensitivity and understanding.

In a time when everybody's trying to be everything, there are more opportunities for feeling guilty over what you're not. Susan fears that standing up for herself might drive the man in her life away. Tom isn't sure whether to lead with his macho image or with his marshmallow heart. The last time he cried in front of his girlfriend she told him to "stop sniveling."

Feeling Guilty for Not Feeling Guilty

Sometimes you give in to temptation and are surprised to find you *don't* feel guilty. The forbidden fruit is tastier than you thought and less coated with self-recrimination. You start feeling guilty because you *don't* feel guilty.

"Reverse Guilt" Psycho-Logic

S. — Survival Assumption.

It's important to feel guilty when I've done something "bad."

E. — Evaluation.

I'm sure I'll feel guilty *if* I am bad (I always do in my imagination).

T. — Tactic.

I was bad but I didn't feel guilty, so I feel guilty for not feeling guilty.

A divorced woman in her mid-thirties told me she was tired of being monogamous. She decided to let herself go and "not feel guilty" about it—to stop "mentally marrying" every man she dated. It took her several weeks to stop feeling guilty for not feeling guilty. She finally found a comfortable compromise between promiscuity and saving herself for Santa Claus.

Guilt Traps

Guilt does serve a useful social function, but a little guilt goes a long way. Most of us end up with more than we need, too generously applied in too many places. The two key questions about guilt are appropriateness and degree. First, did you actually do something that violates your *current adult* sense of right and wrong? Second, is the degree of your guilt proportionate to the damage you did? A twelve-year-old who hanged himself left a note to his parents— "I shot a bluebird so I killed myself." The guilt may have been appropriate—the degree was not.

Exorcising Guilt

If you suffer from guilt that seems justified, maybe it's time to stop doing whatever makes you feel guilty—or get settled with whatever you've already done. If you suffer from guilt that's out of proportion to anything you've done, it may be time to develop a strategy for facing reality.

Guilt can be modified in the same way you modify other Psycho-Logic. You start by identifying the source of your guilt. What "should" or "shouldn't" rule have you broken? It may be something obvious— like dishonesty in a relationship, or it may be more obscure—like feeling guilty for not living up to your own expectations. Once you know what you're guilty of, you may be able to stop doing whatever it is, or you might be able to make up for it in some way. If your guilt is unreasonable, you may be able to replace it with a more appropriate Counter Logic perspective. In that case a Combat Card can be a useful tool. It can remind you to practice a more positive perspective and encourage you to engage in alternative Tactics—such as being *fully* honest with a lover or friend.

Here are some other Counter Logic perspectives that might suggest ways of handling guilt...

Stop shoulding on yourself. Endless rumination about what you "should" or "shouldn't" do only makes you feel bad. If you think you *should* do one thing but *want* to do something else, make a decision, one way or the other, and learn to live with it.

Substitute caring for guilt. It's not necessary to feel guilty every time you say no to your mother. If you love someone, you can pick your own Tactics for expressing that love. If you care for your mother in a way that satisfies you, you don't have to do enough to *totally* satisfy her—and you don't have to feel guilty about it.

How guilty are you? Was whatever you did really that bad or immoral? Did it hurt somebody? What were the catastrophic results that deserve this degree of guilt?

Fit the punishment to the crime. If you have done something that hurt someone, stop wallowing in guilt and figure out a way to make amends. You can't change anything you've done, but you can always do something positive to balance things out a little better. Even if you've killed someone in an automobile accident you can figure out a way to help the family—or some other family. You can't bring anyone back to life, but you can at least make some positive contribution to the living. Most guilt isn't quite that serious, or quite as difficult to balance out.

Put yourself on parole. Decide when you've punished yourself enough. So what if you did tell your wife her nose looks funny? You are sorry for hurting her feelings. You've already apologized. You did the dishes when it wasn't even your turn. How much more guilt is it worth—a day's guilt, a month's, a year's? You decide.

What's the lesson here? A lesson learned is not an experience wasted. If you've learned something from the experience of guilt, further guilt serves no useful purpose.

Grow up. Reconsider your violation in the light of *current* reality. Check out the Psycho-Logic that supports your "shoulds." Are your "should" rules still as valid as when you originally learned them, or are you applying a five-year-old morality to a thirty-five-year-old problem?

The past is dead—so bury it. Guilt often looks backward. No matter how guilty you feel, there's absolutely nothing you can do to correct something that's already happened. You can always do something else—and do it right this time, but no amount of guilt can make up for past mistakes.

Get off the double standard. Check to see if you're applying a double morality. Would you hold a close friend equally guilty for doing the same thing? Many of us are harsher on ourselves than we are on others. Fair is fair.

Establish your own standard. Figure out some Counter Logic and some Tactics that make sense to you—that move your life in a meaningful direction. You don't have to be perfect. All you need is a sense that you're doing something that seems worthwhile *to you*. As long as you're on that path, you're not likely to feel guilty about what you're doing.

14

Anxiety:
Getting Things
Under Control

Worry, bad nerves, anxiety—whatever you call it, it's a common experience.

Anxiety is a feeling that things are out of control, or that they are going to be out of control in the near future. It's your internal fire alarm—your first alert that you're in a situation that may be dangerous. Anxiety can get you ready for "fight or flight" when you're threatened in a dark alley or it can eat a hole in your stomach when a Survival Assumption is chronically threatened. The danger that causes your adrenalin to flow can be physical or Psycho-Logical.

"Anxiety" Psycho-Logic

S. — Survival Assumption.

It's essential (in order to feel secure) to be in control of *all* things, or of *one particular thing* (such as your physical safety, your business success, etc.).

E. — Evaluation.

You feel out of control in one or more essential areas.

T. — Tactics.

Your response and/or attempt to control this crisis situation.
Sample Tactics...
1. Cry, shake, or call your mother.
2. Hide.

3. Give up.
4. Engage in symbolic control (compulsive behavior).
5. Remain in a constant state of panic (i.e., react as if life's monster *really is* on your tail about to gobble you up.).
6., 7., 8. Fight, flight, or manipulate.
9. Tackle the problem regardless of anxiety.

Hidden Assets

Your Psycho-Logic can set you up to be anxious about everything (usually called "generalized anxiety") or about small, seemingly unimportant things. One eighteen-year-old client complained that his girl friend was so anxious about the "ugliness" of her body that it was crippling their relationship. Yet when he first saw her at a high school dance, he was immediately struck by how everyone stared at her figure. He ended up driving her home that night and kissing her good-night on the front porch. He saw her every weekend for the next four months.

He remembered the first time he let his hand slip down past her waist to the round of her buttocks. She didn't resist. Her seventeen-year-old body turned out to be about the most beautiful sight he had ever seen. But that was his opinion. Hers was quite different.

They first made love in his bedroom on a Sunday afternoon. She absolutely insisted that they do it under the covers so he wouldn't have to look at her. But he *wanted* to look at her! They ended up under the covers. Every time after that, the blinds had to be closed and the lights turned off. On one occasion, she got very angry after they chased each other naked around the room, with her turning switches and lamps off and him chasing after her turning them on again. After that she told him if he didn't want to do it *right,* he didn't have to do it at all!

Of course, they had their discussions over the matter. He said he thought she was being dumb. She definitely *was* beautiful. He tried to convince her that if she *really* did love him she wouldn't cover up so much, but that only made her cry. She *did* love him! If she didn't, she wouldn't have gone as far as she had.

What could he say? He wasn't totally unsympathetic. They held each other and cried together. He said he didn't want to lose her. She said she was afraid he wouldn't want her after he saw how ugly she was.

As things turned out in a later conversation, she was especially anxious about a single blemish on her buttocks. There was a birthmark—actually a small ridge of discoloration that ran across both cheeks in two or three thin lines. She admitted she spent hours under a sun lamp trying to tan the lines away, but they never disappeared.

"Blemish" Psycho-Logic

S. — Survival Assumption.

It's important to be beautiful. (Everybody always says I am. It gets me a lot of attention.)

E. — Evaluation.

There's a part of me that's not quite perfect. Therefore, it's ugly. Therefore, *I'm* ugly.

T. — Tactics.

1. Keep my ugly part hidden.
2. Be anxious in a relationship where my secret might be uncovered.

This was a beautiful woman, but that was a much greater pleasure for everyone else than it was for her. She was too busy worrying about the ugliness of her blemishes to appreciate—or even believe—the way other people really saw her.

Last Stand in the Suburbs

Anxiety can occasionally be life-threatening—especially the kind that works on you one drop at a time, like the old Chinese water torture.

I once had a neighbor who lived a "Chicken Little" fear that "something awful" was always about to happen. He had been medically discharged from the navy after having half his stomach removed, along with a bleeding ulcer. It didn't teach him anything. He was still on constant guard. He always checked the two locks on the front door before he went to bed at night, and the deadbolt and double chain on the back door. (It made Psycho-Logic sense that a burglar or rapist would sneak up from behind to avoid a direct attack on the front of the house.)

My neighbor's wife remembers the family ritual every time they went on vacation. They wouldn't be two blocks away from the house when her husband would ask, "Did I lock that front door?" Everyone knew very well he had locked it because they all waited in the car while he banged it, kicked it, turned the key one way and then the other, and then jiggled it to make sure it had caught. Two blocks away he couldn't remember whether he had locked it or not so they all drove back and waited while he checked it again.

It was irrelevant that there hadn't been a house broken into on that street in the twenty-two years the old man lived there. He had seen a burglary report on KJSJ-TV just last week. It was only a matter of time before it happened to him.

My neighbor was friendly enough. He built beautifully designed H.O. train layouts (a Tactic for creating a world he could totally control). He was always adding something new to his collection of train cars and engines, and inviting me over to show them off. I missed him when his second ulcer burst and he bled to death before the ambulance arrived.

I remembered him telling me how his father once bought him a pony but told him to water it every morning. The first time he forgot, he came home from school and found the pony sold. He remembered other losses. During the depression he'd been forced to give up his room so the family could earn a little extra money renting it out. He was only seventeen when his father died of a stroke. That's when he gave up his dream of going to engineering school and reluctantly joined the Navy.

Most of my neighbor's stories were about losing something. No wonder he was on edge all the time. He never knew what might go next. In the end it was his worry that lost him his life.

I helped bear his casket. When we left the old man's house for the funeral parlor, his wife of sixty-three years jiggled the door to make sure it was locked.

"Constant Guard" Psycho-Logic

S. — Survival Assumption.

It's important to be safe and secure.

E. — Evaluation.

Nothing's ever safe or secure. I never know when something important might be snatched away (like my pony, my room, or my father).

T. — Tactics.

1. Be on constant guard (i.e., in a high state of ready anxiety).
2. Lock up everything and check everything twice.
3. Build a miniature world of H.O. trains where everything's perfectly predictable and always under control.
4. Die a death of anxiety and bleeding ulcers.

Risking Failure

Consider the plight of a young mother who is anxious about meeting new people. She recently moved two states away from her parents and the only friends she has ever known.

"It's a little scary not having a single person you can call up or go over and visit. I never really was good at meeting people. I never know what to say. It gives me a knot in my stomach. Sometimes I think it's not worth the effort."

What is it that makes this woman uncomfortable? It isn't being around people—that's exactly what she wants. It's being around *strangers*. It's playing little getting-to-know-you games. It's anxiously waiting to see if they'll accept her. Sometimes, it's being afraid to take the risk of finding out if they will.

Peeling the Onion

It's not this woman's *trying* that's the problem, but rather her *way* of trying. She has no trouble approaching new people—or even saying the first few words to them. Her problem is, what do you say after you say hello?

I suggested Onion-Peeling Tactics— "think of a stranger as an onion (without the tears and the smell of course)."

This onion approach relieved her of the problem of what to say by refocusing her attention on what she wanted to accomplish, and how to go about doing it. Her new goal was not to make a friend—

that put too much pressure on her—or to figure out cute things she could say to impress someone. Her new aim was simply to learn about other people, to draw them out, to make them feel comfortable enough to tell her about themselves and, if possible, to *uncover* something about them that she could genuinely relate to. The "hellos," and the jobs, and the weather were only the first layer of the "onion"—the most superficial. If she could relax enough to get beneath that outside layer, there would always be something in what the other person said or did or in something she already knew about him or her that might lead the conversation to the next inner level. The layers of the onion began to peel away.

Counterfeit interest is hard for anyone to get away with, but most people do appreciate someone who is genuinely interested in learning something *about them,* or something *from them.* Peeling the onion doesn't always work—even if the interest is genuine, but if the potential for a friendship is there, the onion approach is an entry Tactic that has a good chance of opening things up. It might be just the approach an isolated lady needs to get her from the introduction stage to the little-bit-more-familiar level. In the process of discovering more intimate layers, friendships naturally develop—and there's much less anxiety in the process of developing them.

Tactical Approaches

Almost any situation can cause anxiety—from meeting strangers, to a dip in the stock market, to feeling inadequate as a leader. Once you determine those situations that create anxiety in you, you can start developing new Counter Logic or new Tactics to replace those that cause you to feel out of control. A good way to begin is to jot down what's going on when you feel anxious. After you see a pattern emerging, you can make up a Combat Card with your anxiety Tactics on one side and a new set of confidence-building Tactics on the other.

Here's a sampling of what a Combat Card might look like for various kinds of specific anxieties...

Meeting Someone New

• Anxiety Tactic—Put on a show to impress someone (and feel anxious about your performance).

- Confidence Tactic—"Peel the onion" by finding out about the *other* person.

Stock Market Investments

- Anxiety Tactic—Buy the best stocks you can and wait anxiously to see what happens.
- Confidence Tactic—Diversify your holdings and use a ten percent "get-out rule" on any one of them. This allows you to make as much profit as you can without ever losing more than your "get-out" percentage.

Leadership

- Anxiety Tactic—Nervously try to figure out the views of those you lead. Take a poll and make decisions by vote.
- Confidence Tactic—Creatively anticipate what people might want or need. Actually lead by being slightly ahead of them.

Time Scheduling

- Anxiety Tactic—Do things when you get so anxious you can't put them off any longer.
- Confidence Tactic—Keep in mind, or on paper, a list of priorities that focus your attention on what's really important. Narrow the difference between what's important and what you do.

Using Money

- Anxiety Tactic—Spend all you have, beyond necessities, for luxury items and pleasure. Then worry when you don't have enough to buy any more.
- Confidence Tactic—Set up a money account to play "real-world monopoly." The challenge of the game might be fun in itself, and you may end up with a couple of hotels on the Boardwalk (or at least more to spend than you invested).

Workmanship

- Anxiety Tactic—Hurry up and get through whatever you are working on because there are fourteen other things that require your attention.

• Confidence Tactic—When you judge a task to be worthwhile, or potentially enjoyable, *choose* to approach it from the angle of "craftsmanship" rather than "get-donesmanship." Focus on one piece of the job until you are able to take some pride or some joy in what you have accomplished.

Getting Through a Lousy Experience

• Anxiety Tactic—Get it over with.

• Confidence Tactic— "Maximize the gain." Figure out a way to squeeze at least some learning or profit from an otherwise difficult situation. Stop being exasperated over the loss, and start figuring out how to maximize what remains.

Commitment and Involvement

• Anxiety Tactic—Skim nervously across the surface of everything.

• Confidence Tactic—Pick something—anything—and in a more leisurely way, explore it below the surface. Hidden worlds can relax you when you decide to scratch through their crust.

Vacations

• Anxiety Tactic—Plan everything, see everything, and do everything.

• Confidence Tactic—Spend at least a couple of days in one place, without commitments or plans. Relax and get with your inner schedule.

Competition

• Anxiety Tactic—Beat the other guy.

• Confidence Tactic—Improve your own skills by "beating your own record." As you get better at low pressure self-competition, winning over others will flow naturally.

Starting the Day

• Anxiety Tactic—Anticipate all the things that might go wrong that day.

• Confidence Tactic— "Good morning, sunshine."

Arguments

- Anxiety Tactic—Argue the other person out of her opinions.
- Confidence Tactic—Assume that the other person is sincere and correct, given *her* unique experience and point of view. Instead of trying to be right, look for a creative solution that takes *both* your opinions into account—or give the other person your silent "permission to disagree."

Marriage

- Anxiety Tactic—Struggle with each other until your partner gets his or her way or you get yours.
- Confidence Tactic—Cooperate to help each other meet both your needs. Approach marriage as a joint adventure instead of a win-or-lose contest.

Choices

- Anxiety Tactic—Keep jumping back and forth between two solutions—and fretting over both of them.
- Confidence Tactic—What are three other possibilities besides the two I've already got? Most problems don't have to be narrowed down to either-or choices. Black-and-white thinking results from lack of imagination or Psycho-Logic stubbornness.

Being Objective

- Anxiety Tactic—Settle every emotional issue on the spot, while you're still hot and bothered.
- Confidence Tactic—Go ahead and express your feelings, but discuss the issue again when you can approach it from a calmer perspective.

Sexuality

- Anxiety Tactic—Get it up (or get it open), get it in, and get it off.
- Confidence Tactic—Wrap sexuality around layers of *sensuality*. It doubles the pleasure, doubles the fun, and is much more relaxing.

Power

- Anxiety Tactic—Power requires vigilance, winning, and manipulation.
- Confidence Tactic—Power comes from having something to contribute and then finding an effective way to offer it.

Contentment

- Anxiety Tactic—Contentment comes from fighting the external world until you come out on top.
- Confidence Tactic—Contentment comes from living in harmony with a meaningful conception of life.

Fear of Failure

- Anxiety Tactic—Every time I fail, *I* am a failure.
- Confidence Tactic—Even a bitter lesson is not a failure if it brings me one step closer to a solution.

The Ten-Percent Solution

Sometimes dealing with anxiety is as much a matter of readjusting an Evaluation as adding new Tactics. When I was at a psychology convention in San Francisco, I met a psychologist who told me how a change in one of his Evaluations helped him feel a little easier about his professional competence. He said when he first started practicing psychotherapy he took every failure personally, and tended to pile them up one on top of the other, like a growing stack of dirty laundry. After a year of dragging himself out of his house and into his office every day, he finally hit on a "ten-percent solution." One morning while he was lying in bed, wondering if it was worth getting up, he thought about a family he had been treating who told him how grateful they were for his help. The amazing thing was, he believed them—he really had helped that family. Lying in bed, he knew it was the good feeling he got from these obvious successes that kept him going—even though he felt that way only ten percent of the time. He knew his real success rate was probably a lot higher than that. But with ten percent, he was absolutely sure he had helped in some important and positive way. That knowledge felt good.

After he began thinking about this, he started taking more honest satisfaction in the ten-percent success he knew he was getting. Focusing on *that* ten percent kept him from dwelling on the twenty-percent obvious failure, and the big in-between chunk he was never quite sure about. He told me he was still trying for a hundred percent, but that he didn't spend as much time brooding as long as he could count on one honest success in ten. Even that modest rate meant a lot of lives changed in the course of a thirty-year career.

"Failure" Psycho-Logic

S. — Survival Assumption.
It's essential to be an effective therapist (in order to feel good about myself).

E. — Evaluation.
Every time I fail to help a client, *I am a failure.*

T. — Tactic.
Anxiety and self-blame.

"Ten-Percent" Counter Logic

Counter Logic	Ten-percent success has a big effect on a lot of lives.
Counter Tactics	Try for 100 percent—settle for 10 percent (*and feel good about it*).

More Anxiety Counter Logic

Use the energy. That extra flow of anxious adrenalin is supposed to prepare you for something, so prepare yourself to do something with it. If you can attack the problem that's causing the anxiety, do it. If you can't, then attack the quarter-mile track behind the high school gym or attack something else constructive.

Relax! Anxiety tightens you up. When you relax your muscles, some of your nervous energy flows out through your toes and fingers.

Focus on the present. A lot of anxiety comes from anticipating the future or brooding over the past, but you can't change the past and you can't handle the future until it gets here. If something in the past scared you, face it down in the present or let it go. If the future worries you, start practicing how to handle it *right now*.

Psych out the enemy. The more knowledge you have about something the more potential control you have over it. The more control you have, the less anxiety. Spend your time gathering information instead of worrying and wondering.

One small step at a time. Maybe you can't climb a ladder all the way to the roof, but you can probably climb the first step, and maybe the one after that, and perhaps one more. Tomorrow maybe you can do another one. Who knows how high you can climb?

Have a shootout. Face your fear! Look it in the eye. Running from fear often keeps it alive. When you stop running and stare it down, it may not be as scary as you thought.

You can't or you won't? You *can't* face what makes you anxious or you *won't* face it? Think how good you'd feel if you faced it anyway. It might be a big load off your shoulders. Why not get it settled once and for all?

Give your anxiety a name. What's the name of the thing that's scaring you—Martha, Old Man Money, Responsibility? When you have a name for it maybe you can learn to live with it on more familiar and less threatening terms.

Grab the silver lining. Stop spending your life cowering under the rainbow waiting for the thunder to strike. Reach up and grab some of the color.

15

Depression: Licking Your Wounds and Putting Your Losses Behind You

Helen was depressed. She stopped keeping her exercise journal when she found herself writing about the aches and pains of a fifty-two-year-old woman. She had once been an active athlete—played soccer in high school and tennis all through college. She had started jogging way before it was fashionable and kept it up for nearly nine years. After her back started hurting her she tried to "run through the pain," but her doctor told her she was jarring her spine too much and would have to give jogging up altogether. After all her years of fighting to stay in shape, Helen suddenly let go of everything. She saw no sense in fighting a losing battle against age. Depression took the place of her exercise routine.

Growing older had never been pleasant for Helen. Twenty-seven was her idea of a perfect age. She had always joked that she wouldn't mind dying as long as she could grow old and die young. She had hoped that her dedication and exercise—especially her jogging—would be her fountain of youth. Now the fountain was shut off—just when age was creeping up on her more relentlessly than ever. It just didn't seem fair—maybe for someone else, but not for her.

The Psycho-Logic of Depression

Depression results from an actual or symbolic loss, along with feelings of helplessness to regain that loss. The loss can be external, such as the loss of youth or the death of a loved one; or it can be internal, such as the loss of meaning or purpose.

Depression Psycho-Logic

S. — Survival Assumption.

It's important (in order to feel useful, worthwhile, or important) to have a certain thing as part of my life, or as part of something I'm working for in life.

E. — Evaluation.

I have (a) lost that something or (b) lost a sense that I can ever attain it.

T. — Tactics.

I give up. I feel helpless. Nothing seems worth having (if I can't have *that*).

Razor Blade Tactics

Sometimes a loss can be so devastating that life itself no longer seems worthwhile. I once treated a twelve-year-old boy who slashed his wrists after his dog died. The boy had moved to town six months earlier but had not made a single friend at school or in the neighborhood. The dog had been his only companion. He wanted either to be dead and end his loneliness or to be with his dog in heaven. He didn't care which.

Suicide is not the lowest form of depression. Some depressives sink so low they don't have enough energy to kill themselves. Suicide often occurs when someone's coming up from depression. One gunshot victim told his doctor, "As soon as I was feeling better I realized things were just as bad as I thought they were!"

Depression doesn't usually lead to suicide. It more often leads to a kind of walking death—a comatose condition—a major slowdown of life functions. Depression saps your strength, drains your energy, ruins your appetite, and dampens your spirit. When it's long enough and deep enough, it robs you of everything that makes life seem worth living. You may continue to go through the motions but zest for life disappears.

It's easy to understand how the collapse of a family business or the death of a father can lead to depression, but a lot of depression comes from the loss of a dream—or realization that a dream didn't turn out the way it was supposed to. A woman who had been to her high school reunion was depressed for a month after her return. The trip reminded her so much of what she had hoped for in those days. When she told her husband she felt like a failure her husband tried to reassure her that she had done okay. "I know," she told him, "but I didn't set out to do *okay!*"

The Fire Dampens

There was no major disaster in Jerry's life. There wasn't even a minor one. He was married and had two kids. He was well respected at work and had slowly made his way to the top of middle management. He watched the evening news every night at 7 o'clock, took three weeks vacation in the summer, still had an eight percent mortgage and was in perfect health, so why was he depressed?

It wasn't anything that came on suddenly. Over the past year or two he just felt slowly drained—washed out, like an old shirt that had been through the laundry too many times. His spirit and energy were gone. Twenty years ago he would have been ecstatic to dream of the success he had made of himself. But having it now didn't bring him the satisfaction he thought it would. The three-story house that had once excited him so much was now just a place to watch TV and wait for the next leak in the plumbing. And his marriage? Being married to the same person twenty-two years had lost its glamour. Not that his marriage was bad. He just didn't know if he was in love anymore. As for his kids, he had to admit he *did* love them—even though they were a nuisance half the time and an outrageous expense. His plan to start a college fund was already six years behind schedule.

The biggest disappointment was his career. The job that had once fascinated him—that had even scared him a little—was now nothing but grind and routine. It was about as challenging as blowing his nose—and the line for promotion was three miles long. He had long ago settled into shuffling papers from the in box to the out box.

Jerry's whole life was a dull routine. He had acquired all the *things* he had once hoped for but didn't have the feeling of satisfaction and accomplishment that was supposed to go with them. Worst of all, there was nothing left that seemed worth accomplishing.

Jerry's "Faded Adventure" Psycho-Logic

S. — Survival Assumption.

It's important to have excitement in life—something to look forward to and work toward.

E. — Evaluation.

Life was exciting when I was first dating and starting a career. Now that I have everything, there's nothing left to excite me.

T. — Tactic.

The slow grind of maintenance, routine, and chronic depression.

Feeling Hopeless

You can lose a lot of things and not be affected by the loss. It's losing something Psycho-Logically important that causes depression—whether it be your three-year-old son or your sense of achievement. It's especially a permanent loss that leaves you feeling helpless in the face of your inability to bring it back.

When you're severely depressed there's a great temptation to exaggerate the effect of your loss—to wallow in your misery. If you lose your only friend you start thinking you'll *never* have another friend again—or at least not a close one. Your prediction of future loneliness and your self-blame make you feel even worse...

"Poor Me" Psycho-Logic

S. — Survival Assumption.

It's essential to be accepted by others—or, at least, *one* other.

E. — Evaluation.

I'm too (fat, ugly, dumb, quiet, etc.). That's why no one likes me.

T. — Tactic.

Mope around the house feeling miserable because I'm such an unlikable person (even *I* don't like me).

Doubts about your competence permeate your thinking. If you don't have the power to deal with your present loss, how are you ever going to generate future satisfactions? And if you start out expecting a negative outcome, where are you going to get the energy to engage in behavior that might refute your expectation?

After Dave and Betty separated, Dave didn't care about anything. He never expected to be happy again.

Dave's "One-and-Only" Psycho-Logic

S. — Survival Assumption.

It's essential to have someone to love and care for me in order to be happy.

E. — Evaluation.

I was in love with Betty but she left me. Since there's no one else like Betty, I'll never be in love again and *never be happy*.

T. — Tactics.

1. Give up. Do only what's required.
2. Stay depressed.

Surviving the Prison Blues

You get depressed when you lose something or someone Psycho-Logically important. And yet you have little control over many of life's gains or losses. You are often a prisoner of losses beyond your control, yet you can always choose the way you handle these losses—at least within yourself. Many prisoners who have lost their freedom—sometimes with the threat of death hanging over them—have found an internal perspective to help them through their ordeal.

After his release from jail, the "silent" Watergate burglar, Gordon Liddy, repeated a line from the philosophy of Nietzsche that had kept him going during his imprisonment— "What doesn't kill me makes me stronger." Liddy had found a compatible Counter Logic—or way of thinking about things—that both justified his Watergate involvement and made his prison existence a little more bearable. By seeing himself as a martyr and super-spy hero—and finding a Nietzschean way of thinking about it—he was able to remain untouched by massive evidence to the contrary.

   This need for a perspective in difficult times is close to the experience of Victor Frankl, a Jewish psychiatrist, who spent most of World War II as a prisoner in a Nazi concentration camp. In his later writing about that time, Frankl noted that those who were not directly killed by the Germans died a slower death of despair and discouragement, unless they were able to find—*and keep in mind*—some life purpose beyond their prison walls. Frankl survived by developing his theory of existential therapy, which touched the bare bones of human existence and helped him tend to other prisoners who needed a reason to live.

   The Birdman of Alcatraz was another prisoner who survived on depression and anger until his concern for the well-being of "caged-up canaries" turned his whole life around and occupied his attention for the next forty years.

   All of us are, to some degree, prisoners of ourselves and our circumstances. We are each locked within a certain span of years and an aging process over which we have very little control. There are added limitations of physical and human resources that sometimes keep us from getting or keeping those things that are crucially important to us. Much of what we want is in conflict with what others want, or in conflict with other things that *we* want. But even beyond these real world limitations, we often attach additional obstacles by the views we take of what we get—or what we lose.

   It is always possible to handle the loss with grace by dealing with it in a way that leaves your pride intact, or by using a loss to help you find new depth and meaning in life. Developing grace under fire—whatever your loss—is not a bad Counter Logic to hold onto.

Growing with Age

   By the time Helen sought professional help for her depression she was already tired of being depressed. She had been moping over her lost youth for over six months. "Where do I go from here?" she wanted to know. I told her she had already started—that she had already gone through most of her mourning. It was up to her to decide where to go next.

   We talked about her feelings about aging and death—or, rather, living. She *was* getting older. Her body *was* slowly falling apart. She *was* losing some of her energy—her youthful passion. There was no denying these physical and emotional realities, but on the other hand she was gaining serenity, she was less neurotically driven, better able to look at things with a caring but dispassionate view. She was more objective. Her emotions were not as intense at fifty-two as they were at thirty-two, but they were deeper and steadier. Her body didn't perform as well or look as good as it did twenty years ago, but much of her strength remained and she had long ago learned that endurance was as much a matter of concentration as age.

Now that Helen had confronted her own mortality, perhaps her life could be richer in some ways, more precious. Perhaps it was time for her to stop crying over spilt milk and learn to appreciate and savor what she had—and what was still being added.

Helen's "Fountain of Youth" Psycho-Logic

S. — Survival Assumption.

It's essential to be young and athletic (the need for physical survival, stimulation, and attention).

E. — Evaluation.

As long as I can stay young and vigorous, I can meet all these needs.

T. — Tactics.

1. Jogging, athletics, and physical exercise to keep myself youthful.
2. Total collapse of effort (depression) when the aches, pains, and wrinkles eat away at the muscles.

Helen's "Life Appreciation" Counter Logic

Counter Logic	Each stage of life subtracts something but *adds* something else. Appreciate whatever stage I'm in.
Counter Tactics	1. Keep up my exercise at a more moderate level. (Stay as attractive as I can *for the age I am.*)
	2. Explore the deeper things in life—the things I can understand better now—perhaps religion or philosophy.
	3. Spend more time on the little things that mean so much—my flower garden, my grandchild, summer sunsets in back of my house.

The New Adventures of Jerry

Jerry had reached a plateau in his life. He achieved what he had set out to achieve—the status, the business success, the family—but it wasn't enough to satisfy him. He was depressed because he expected success to bring him more. It hadn't, and yet there had been a time when all these things meant something to him—when they seemed worth working for. Maybe it was all an illusion—like chasing rainbows. He remembered thinking about chasing rainbows when he was a kid—about finding the pot of gold. Maybe he needed a new rainbow to chase. So what if there wasn't a pot of gold at the end? The fun was in the adventure of getting there. It was the challenge—the race—not the trophy. Jerry *had* collected a lot of trophies, but now all that his trophies collected was dust. Maybe it was time to start thinking about his next adventure instead of complaining that the trophies didn't do anything for him.

Jerry's "New Adventure" Counter Logic

Counter Logic	When one adventure is over, sign up for a new one.
Counter Tactics	1. Consider taking up a real adventure—a new challenge (maybe hang gliding, sheer cliff rock climbing or kayaking).
	2. Develop a family adventure in which my family can participate (like backpacking the national parks or building a rustic cabin in the mountains).

Depression Counter Logic

You can't always prevent a Psycho-Logic loss, but you *can* do something about the depression it generates. Here is some Counter Logic that might help you put your situation in perspective and suggest useful Counter Tactics...

Share the blame. There's always a tendency to come down too hard on yourself when you lose something important—to swallow all the blame yourself. That's usually an exaggeration of your own importance. If your husband walked out on you it was at least part of his doing—no matter how hard you were to live with. If you didn't get your promotion, maybe the person who did get it really was better than you—or maybe she just had more seniority. The fact that some people are better or that there is a seniority system *is not your fault,* so blame the system, and then figure out how to use it to *your* benefit.

Keep buzzing. When you're depressed you stop everything. That's the worse thing you can do. It gives you too much time to think about your miseries, and while you are doing nothing, other things start falling apart. You don't need another collapse to get you depressed even more. When you keep active, things are more likely to happen—even some good things. A bee that keeps buzzing makes honey whether its heart is in it or not.

If you don't feel like doing anything, organize something. If you don't have the energy to tackle a project, organize one. Gather information. Get something ready to go. If it's organized, it'll take less energy when you do feel like starting.

Think small. Plan small routine tasks that give you an immediate sense of accomplishment—something that will focus your attention on the here-and-now instead of your recent loss. Cut the grass, do the dishes, make your bed, jog a mile—anything that can be totally completed in a short amount of time. These kinds of tasks directly challenge your "helpless" Psycho-Logic. The feeling that you *can do something* is much more important than whatever you do.

Wait actively. If you're waiting for the next promotion to develop, or waiting for your girl friend to come to her senses, do something while you are waiting. Most depressions don't last forever. Situations change and you begin to feel different about them after awhile. Waiting is sometimes exactly the right thing to do—particularly if you make a decision to wait for a specified amount of time—say a couple of weeks or a few months. While you are waiting, you can keep busy with things you've been putting off—or things that might pay off in some meaningful way.

Sleep a lot. People naturally sleep more when they're depressed. It's a way to escape depression—a minivacation—one less hour to worry. Why fight it? Sleep when you feel like sleeping—and keep active when you don't.

Change something. Go somewhere new or do something different. Plan nondestructive escapes. Use emotional music to lift your mood. The stimulation of something new invites involvement—and involvement works against the detachment of depression. When you do something that grabs your attention, you sometimes forget what you are depressed about—at least for awhile.

Talk it out. Talk things over with a friend. Since the friend isn't likely to have the same Psycho-Logic as you, his or her objectivity may help you gain a new perspective, and even if it doesn't, studies show that talking things out with someone who listens automatically helps relieve depression.

One bad inning doesn't lose a ball game. A team that gives up every time it gets behind never comes from behind. A game is never over until the final score is in. Challenge yourself to keep going even when you're behind—even when you have taken an important loss, and if you do end up losing, lose courageously.

Challenge your Psycho-Logic. Is this particular job or this particular person *really essential* for your happiness? Is there no other possible job or relationship that could fit in your life in a significant or meaningful way? Is it possible that something or someone else—not yet known to you—could bring you equal or even greater satisfaction? Could this loss be a disguised opportunity to try something different?

Develop a new dream—or resurrect an old one. Dream again. Use positive time projection. Where do you want to be five years from now? Simply coming up with another possibility helps relieve depression. Then devlop an action plan around your dream. Figure out a schedule of daily attainable goals. Take things in small steps that guarantee small successes. Then take another step. Who knows where you will end up?

A happy life is a collection of happy moments. Sure you've had some bad ones, so now you go out and get some good ones to balance things out.

16

Relationships:
Psycho-Logic Fits
and Misfits

The fulfillment of most Psycho-Logic requires at least one other person. You can't be loved and attended to unless there is someone loving and attentive around. Power over no one is no power at all. Stimulation often requires someone to do the stimulating, or to be stimulated with. While you are sizing up a stranger to see how he might meet your Psycho-Logic needs, he is scrutinizing you to see how you might meet his. If you both pass the initial screening, the possibility is open for a Psycho-Logic Contract (sometimes simply called a Relationship Contract).

A relationship contract is an implied understanding about how the Psycho-Logic of two people will be played out between them—especially the Tactics they will use in maintaining their relationship.

Congruent or Incongruent Contracts

Psycho-Logic contracts are said to be congruent if both parties are satisfied with how they operate. They are incongruent if one party wants something from the other that he or she is not getting. A contract may start out congruent but end up incongruent if the Psycho-Logic of one person changes without a corresponding change in the other's Psycho-Logic.

Louise was a late-blooming adolescent who needed someone to lean on. She married Doug when she was eighteen and he was twenty-seven. They had a workable contract until she turned twenty-five and developed a sudden urge to be on her own. By that time Louise saw Doug as too much like her father. A contract that had worked for an eighteen-year-old girl no longer worked for a twenty-five-year-old woman.

Hard or Soft Contracts

Just as Pyscho-Logic can be "hard" or "soft" so can Psycho-Logic contracts. In a soft contract an individual has very little emotional investment in the outcome. You may think someone is your friend—and perhaps she is while you are with her—but she forgets you quickly when you're gone and, when you return, you find you've been easily replaced.

In a hard Psycho-Logic contract the individual stakes her self-Evaluation on the outcome of the contract. She becomes so dependent on the other person to meet her Psycho-Logic needs that she feels she cannot "survive" unless the contract is fulfilled. If Dorothy relies on John to provide her life with structure, she falls apart when he doesn't provide it. If Richard needs someone to care for, or to argue with, his life seems empty without the object of his affection or confrontation.

Relationships work best when they are flexible—somewhere between the extremes of hardness and softness. Flexibility exists when both parties are willing to bend somewhat to meet the other person's needs, but not so far that their own Psycho-Logic needs are left unmet.

Sometimes one person seeks a hard contract while the other wants a soft one. ("I need you desperately!" with someone who feels "It's pleasant to have you around, but don't expect too much.") This can be especially painful to the hard contractor, but both parties eventually become uncomfortable and even hostile over this kind of incongruence. ("Why don't you love me?" clashes with "Stop making so many demands!")

Kinds of Contracts

Since all Psycho-Logic comes from the eight basic needs, it's not surprising that relationships are a way of meeting one or more of these needs. Everyone requires some fulfillment in each of these crucial areas, but a relationship contract is based on those one or two needs that a particular relationship *cannot survive without*. It's the emotional glue that holds a relationship together. When the emotional glue dries up, the relationship falls apart. A lifelong relationship based on envy and power might not survive a sudden switch to love and tenderness. A loving relationship changes or dissolves when the love it is based on no longer exists.

The current Psycho-Logic needs of each party determine the kind of relationship contract two people attempt to establish.

1.—Need for Physical Survival

Cave Man clubbed a saber-toothed tiger to save Cave Woman from a saber-tooth bite. Cave Woman kept lookout while Cave Man rested. A large part of their relationship was based on life-and-death survival. Modern Man builds Nautilus muscles to admire in his mirror while Modern Woman finds ways to bring home her own bacon. We've come a long way. Few of today's relationships are based on literal survival. But there are exceptions.

> **Parental Contract** — I'll feed you and change you and keep you alive if you _____ (stay alive, respond to my caring, meet important Psycho-Logic needs, etc.).

First mothers frequently get depressed after spending a few weeks expending all their energy and getting little back in return. It's often a great delight and a needed reward when a new mother first sees her baby smile. Like any relationship contract, a mother needs something in return for her efforts.

> **Handicap Contract** — I'll be your _____ (eyes, ears, feet, etc.) if you _____ (meet one or more of my Psycho-Logic needs).

Handicapped people go through a state of resenting their need to be cared for. The caretaker comes to be too great a reminder of their disability. Only when they learn to truly accept their handicap can they accept the person who loves and cares for them regardless of it.

> **Death Contract** — I'll literally *kill you* if you _____ (run around with another man, refuse to give me a divorce or will me all your money, etc.).

2—Need to Be Loved and Cared for

Even the crusty among us need some love and caring—a little TLC once in awhile. Those who seem immune to tenderness are often protecting themselves from the loss of this very quality. ("I'll keep myself from losing what I really need by never getting it.")

Love and caring are such universal human needs they are often at the heart of a relationship contract.

TLC Contract — I'll love and care for you if you love and care for me.

This is a straightforward trade-off contract often seen at the beginning of a romantic relationship. It's the kind of contract that can lead to true companionship if the caring continues after the love cools.

Can't Live Without You Contract — I'll love and care for you if you promise never to leave me.

This is a desperation contract in which one or both parties feel their lives would be meaningless without this particular partner. I once counseled a middle-aged man who told me he was in love for the first time in his life—not with his wife but with his girl friend. He *knew* he would never fall in love like this again. His dilemma was not his girl friend but what to do with his wife.

Love for Life Contract — I'll love and care for you as long as you _____ (dominate me, stimulate me, or meet some other Psycho-Logic need).

In this kind of relationship someone is loved because he or she meets an important Psycho-Logic need. To the extent that each party's Tactics actually meet the other's needs, a mutually satisfying contract develops. If, for example, you have the need to be around someone who seems "strong," that's exactly the quality that's likely to stimulate your feelings of love. If this "strong person" needs someone to admire him or respond to his strength—qualities that you provide—he is likely to feel good about being around you.

3—Need for Attention and Approval

Rodney Dangerfield never gets enough respect. That's another way of saying he never gets enough approval. I once treated a physician who told me, "I work my butt off but no one ever seems to

notice!" He was desperately searching for a relationship with someone who would notice.

Performance Contract — I'll agree to put on a performance
if you'll agree to applaud (i.e., notice me).

In this kind of contract one party agrees to be the performer
(doer, achiever, story-teller, etc.) while the other agrees to be an
enthusiastic audience. This is usually a one-way contract in which
the roles are seldom reversed. It may involve a wife who feels her
husband already gets enough attention at the office and should spend
his time at home paying attention to her. When her husband is
inattentive, her idea of a contract is violated. She feels cheated.

Poison Arrow Contract — I'll *disapprove* of you if you
disapprove of me (and we'll both give each other a lot of
attention over it).

Wayne's state police career is the centerpiece of his life. His wife
Faye resents his gun, his night and weekend hours, and—most of
all—his dedication. For his part, Wayne resents his wife's inflexibility
and lack of support. They don't outwardly argue much but their
disapproval and disappointment hang in the air over the dinner table
and invade nearly every corner of their relationship.

Mutual Interest Contract — I'll pay attention to your legiti-
mate (and reasonable) needs if you'll pay attention to
mine.

This is a fairly even sharing of attention, recognition, or
approval. Although the amount of attention may get a little lopsided
for brief periods, it tends to even out in the long run. Jerry takes pride
in his fish tank; Amy openly encourages Jerry's enthusiasm. She
doesn't excuse herself from meeting Jerry's need for attention
because she "hates fish." Jerry shows an equal interest in Amy's life
and activities.

4—Need for Stimulation

Some people like to sit on the back porch and watch the grass
grow, while others get bored if they don't go dancing three nights a
week. A mismatch in the need for stimulation is a frequent cause of
discomfort among friends and companions. It's hard to run a race
together when the pace of the runners is different.

A client once told me she went on a sailing trip with two friends who hadn't spoken to her since they hit dry land. The friends couldn't understand why she wanted to Calypso on the islands until 4 a.m. every night, while they wanted to go to bed at 11:30. She told me, "You really get to know people when you are stuck on a boat with them. Can you imagine living with someone who likes to go to bed at 11:30?" Her friends probably couldn't imagine living with someone who didn't.

> **Circus Monkey Contract** — I'll make your life exciting (by keeping you off balance, by acting crazy, planning trips to Pago-Pago, running for the U.S. Senate, etc.) if you...
> a. do the same for me.
> b. *don't* do the same for me (I'll be the clown and you provide the laughter).
> c. do something *else* for me (I'll provide the stimulation while you provide the money, the stability in the relationship, or whatever).

At its extreme, this is a George and Martha contract in Edward Albee's *Who's Afraid of Virginia Woolf.* George and Martha agreed to dig each other to the emotional core in a contest to see who could get under the skin the deepest and draw the most blood.

> **Birthday Cake Contract** — I'll light Roman candles on your birthday if you light Roman candles on mine (a limited mutual stimulation contract).

This is a relationship between two people who use the excitement and stimulation of each other to meet their mutual need for stimulation. It may be the Flying Fontonies or the traveling Mahonies. If a wife likes to travel and her husband is a coin collector, they schedule a lot of their traveling around coin exhibitions. If a husband provides most of the sexual stimulation, the wife might plan evenings at the theater or weekend excursions.

5—Need for Structure

Contracts based on structure tend to be rigid—that's usually the point of them. Each participant wants to know *exactly* what to expect from the other. Everything's expected to run with precision. When it doesn't there's a major catastrophy.

Chief Conductor Contract — I'll make all the decisions if you agree to follow them (without too much rebellion).

This is a parent-child kind of contract where one of the parties establishes the bounds of the relationship and the other is expected to stay within them. The submissive partner often *asks* for instructions—or waits for them. Occasional rebellion is allowed in order to let off steam, as long as no fundamental changes are made in the agreement.

Mutual Decision Contract — I'll structure things in my area(s) if you structure things in yours.

This is a mature contract of shared equality. Some decisions are made jointly, while others are assigned by expertise or willingness. Harry does the laundry and Mary does the bills. If Mary complains that her blouses aren't being hung up properly, Harry starts hanging them the way she likes. If Harry complains there's not enough money at the end of the month, Mary shows him the bills. When they have their differences, they skip the defense and work them out.

6—Need for Self-Reliance

How can you have an intimate relationship and still be independent? That's an agonizing question these days. Most people are not looking for hermitlike isolation. They're looking for some sort of *inter*dependence. A relationship that involves sharing but still leaves them something to exclusively call their own.

Distant Roommate Contract — I'll leave you alone if you'll leave me alone.

This is a contract in which the parties agree to share expenses and chores but very little else. Sometimes a marriage deteriorates to this functional level. A married couple may get tired of each other— they may develop compelling interests outside the marriage. After thirty years of married life, Lenora lies in bed dreaming of romance the way it was twenty-five years ago. Leon faces the other wall and dreams of the secretary across from his office.

Off Limits Contract — I'll leave you alone in *your private areas* if you leave me alone in mine.

In this contract, one party agrees not to deal with the other party in a *certain restricted area*. Joe and Charlie have been friends for years even though Joe can't stand tennis and Charlie can't live without it. They simply never talk about it. Tony has a high-pressure job at the telephone company. When his day is over he likes to leave his troubles at the office. He rarely talks about work at home. Wednesday is Harriet's night out with her friends. It's her time to get away from husband, home, and children. Harriet and Tony respect each other's personal space.

7—Need for Power

Power is sometimes disguised as "leadership" the "man-of-the-house" or "just-seeing-to-it-that-things-get-done." Power in relationships can be shared, dispensed, fought for, or requested. Psycho-Logic can lead one person to search for someone to tell him what to do. It can lead another to search for someone who will submit to her authority.

Domination Contract — I'll control if you'll submit.

When I asked twelve-year-old Jamie who was "in charge" in her family she immediately said, "Mom. Whenever I ask Dad if I can do something he always says, 'Go ask your Mom.'" "Who picks the kind of car you buy or says where you live?" "Mom does, then she asks Dad what he thinks."

Rebel Contract — I'll attempt to control you if you resist.

In this contract one party agrees to set up regulations (or expectations) while the other party agrees to try and break them. A father tells his fifteen-year-old daughter she *will not* smoke pot. The daughter leaves a couple of joints on her dresser to show her father *she will*.

Jeb and the Colonel

Jeb saw himself as a city dweller transplanted to the country. He told me he was having real problems "getting along with the farmers." He described himself as the kind of person who smoked marijuana whenever he wanted, chased naked women around his yard in thunderstorms, and invited people over to dance in the kitchen while he hummed on a comb wrapped in waxed paper. It all seemed more than a little strange to the folks in rural Delaware. Jeb couldn't seem to make a friend. He had a high need for stimulation—for a bit of the unconventional. He was proud of being different, but he didn't want to be different alone.

Jeb's "Fantasy Island" Psycho-Logic

S. — Survival Assumption.

It's essential to be different—to stir up some excitement in life (need for stimulation).

E. — Evaluation.

My life is exciting when I do what I feel like doing.

T. — Tactics.

1. Spit in the wind just to see if I can duck before it hits me.
2. Other adventure-seeking Tactics (that bother people but don't really hurt them).

Jeb's closest neighbor was a retired Marine colonel. The colonel was constantly spying on Jeb through his World War II binoculars. Jeb once spied back through a toilet paper tube. After that incident the Colonel was more careful to camouflage himself behind his dining room curtain.

The Colonel's "Spit-and-Polish" Psycho-Logic

S. — Survival Assumption.

Control is an essential element in life.

E. — Evaluation.

I keep things under control through discipline and military rigor.

T. — Tactic.

Keep my shoes shined, my shoulders back, and my neighbors in line.

Jeb and the colonel had rather strong feelings about each other. They had a relationship contract based on each playing out his own Psycho-Logic. Jeb had an audience for his unconventionality—

someone to snub his nose at—and the colonel had an undisciplined neighbor who clearly needed controlling.

This is a good example of how relationship contracts are negotiated in a step-by-step behavioral sequence. Jeb sees the colonel glancing at him with a disapproving eye and seizes on the opportunity to flaunt his unconventionality. Like any good soldier, the colonel takes up the challenge and begins his reconnaissance. They see in each other a way to play out their Psycho-Logic needs. The colonel sets out to prove that he can somehow influence Jeb's behavior and Jeb sets out to prove he can get away with "just being himself." They develop their Tactics and go to work on each other.

Slow Dance Contract — We'll take turns leading with a gentle hand.

This is an agreement to lead when your partner accepts your invitation. It's an above-board choice of leadership that changes as the situation changes. It's a back-and-forth flow of power that is always open to renegotiation. Phillip admits that he's currently going through some Psycho-Logic changes that drain a lot of his energy. He doesn't feel like making major decisions at this moment in his life. Mary Ann agrees to take charge of the family decisions—at least temporarily.

8—Need for Accomplishment/Achievement

Blue Ribbon Rooster (or Prize Hen) Contract — I'll agree to achieve something important if you agree *not to*. (I'll be very upset and jealous if you do!)

In this kind of contract there's room for only one champion— one blue ribbon. Any glory shared is glory lost. If Vicki is noted for her beauty, it's important that George be noted for nothing—or at least nothing important. If James Houghten III has a reputation as the best lawyer in the county, Mrs. James Houghten III should simply *and exclusively* be proud of her role as Mrs. Houghten III.

Twin-Engine Contract — I'll agree to achieve something "important" if you agree to do likewise. (I don't want to be the only one "contributing" in this relationship.)

In this kind of contract it's important to *both* parties that *both* parties achieve. A stock broker client told me, "I don't want to stick around with someone who has nothing to offer. I'm serious about what I do and I respect that in someone else." Another client saw it from a different angle ... "I know I'm satisfied with what I'm doing when my girl friend's achievement doesn't make me jealous. Things work out best when we're both achieving something."

Good Matches

The best way to increase satisfaction in your relationships is to choose those people whose Psycho-Logic complements yours. Once you know what your Psycho-Logic is, you're in a much better position to know which combinations work best with it. Figure 1 gives you an idea of how the eight Psycho-Logic needs match or mismatch.

Relationship Counter Logic

If you are having trouble with a particular relationship, or with relationships in general, you might find it helpful to consider a new Counter Logic perspective—along with whatever Tactics it might suggest. Here are some Counter Logic possibilities ...

Peel the Onion. The more interest you show in someone else, the more interest that person is likely to show in you. The more you get to know about someone, the more you'll be able to see if his or her Psycho-Logic fits comfortably with yours.

Pull Down Their Pants. Even the President pulls his pants down in the bathroom. So do Phil Donahue, Jane O'Conner, Wonder Woman, and the Prince of Wales. Famous people and authority figures are just people who occasionally exercise authority and do famous things—often without knowing why. They all have their Psycho-Logic and their Tactics for trying to fulfill it. If you find a way to meet their needs in a way that meets some of your own, a Psycho-Logic contract will easily develop. When you are a little scared to approach people who seem more important, famous, or heroic than you, think of them with their pants down.

Look for "No-Lose" Solutions. Problems in relationships are seldom questions of "right" or "wrong"—even though people heatedly defend the "correctness" of their Psycho-Logic over someone else's. A

FIGURE 1

	PHYSICAL SURVIVAL	LOVED AND CARED FOR	ATTENTION & APPROVAL	STIMULATION	STRUCTURE	SELF-RELIANCE	EXERT POWER OVER OTHERS	ACCOMPLISHMENT
PHYSICAL SURVIVAL	Cooperate to point of starvation. Then eat each other. (Plane crash deaths)							↑
NEED TO BE LOVED AND CARED FOR	Physical Survival usually takes precedence over any other need	O.K. if both willing to trade	X	The high need for stimulation often results in an untrustworthy relationship.	X	As Loved & Cared for demands more, Self-reliance withdraws.	X	Complementary if the relationship is part of what needs accomplishing
NEED FOR ATTENTION & APPROVAL		Conflicting needs can create feelings of emotional abandonment	Potential for jealous rivalry	X	A & A can get losts of attention by maintaining structures and schedules	X	Potential for A & A to be manipulated by power of flattery	X
NEED FOR STIMULATION		X	Stimulation is often too busy to give the needed attention and approval	Can be a good match unless the stimulation required is with other people	X	A good match if parties don't go entirely off into their own little worlds	X	Works when the accomplishment is stimulating and inclusive. Doesn't work when it's dull.

	NEED FOR STRUCTURE	NEED FOR SELF RELIANCE	NEED TO EXERT POWER OVER OTHERS	NEED FOR ACCOMPLISHMENT
NEED FOR STRUCTURE	A workable contract if structure in the relationship is important to both	Usually unable to live together or truly understand each other	A good match if Tactics are similar, a disaster if not.	A clash of wills
NEED FOR SELF RELIANCE	Self-reliance usually unwilling to give in to need for structure	A good working relationship with little intimacy	Self-reliance may not understand why anyone would need so much attention and approval	Often ignore each other even though the form of the relationship gives some comfort
NEED TO EXERT POWER OVER OTHERS	Complementary needs – just a question of effective Tactics	A disastrous combination. Totally opposite needs.	A constant power struggle unless one concedes in the relationship	Frustration for Power when Stimulation doesn't come under control
NEED FOR ACCOMPLISHMENT	Can work well in giving direction and stability for both	OK unless Accomplishment is a workaholic with no time left for attention giving	Workable if the accomplishment of one translates into power for the other	Satisfying if work is together – otherwise two different worlds

salesman who counts on relaxing at home after a long day on the road may come home to a wife who wants to go out for dinner just to get away from the house. This is not a problem of right or wrong. It's a problem of meeting the needs of two people coming from two different perspectives. Winning an argument about who is "right" settles nothing and, even worse, breeds resentment in the relationship. So why not skip the argument and start looking for the no-lose solution that has something in it for everyone?

Give Them a Pink Elephant. Love or caring must be expressed in a way the recipient understands and believes in. A husband who occasionally says "I love you," but who never expresses love through physical affection or thoughtfulness is likely to have his sincerity doubted—no matter how genuine his feelings. A man who puts great stock in sexuality is likely to wonder if his wife cares about him if she constantly excuses herself because *she's* not interested. If you love someone who is crazy about pink elephants, you express your love by giving him or her pink elephants *whether they turn you on or not.* If that person is also giving you your pink elephant, you have a genuine caring relationship.

Lose Your Glass Slipper in Front of the Right Castle. Just like shoes, relationships that don't fit hurt you more than they get you anywhere. When you know your shoe size it's a lot easier to find a pair that does fit, and when you understand your Psycho-Logic it's a lot easier to find a relationship that complements it.

Cultivate Your Garden. All relationships require work. The more intimate they are, the more work they require. When the Psycho-Logic conditions are right, the more you cultivate your relationship, the more it grows.

17

Sexuality: The Ultimate Sensual Experience

Sexuality rarely stands alone. It is embedded within the Psycho-Logic of a relationship. In fact, a person's Psycho-Logic is often played out most blatantly in his or her sexual life.

Down to Basics

Ellen said what most women suspect, "A man hides better when he's dressed than when he's naked. Get him in bed a couple of times and you find out his secrets." Ellen wanted to discover a man's secrets. She was ready for a serious relationship. When she met a dentist at a friend's house she was hoping this would be it. She found herself instantly captivated by his sensitive manner and his desire to know everything about her. In less than a month she was dropping hints about marriage and driving halfway across town to bring him a hot lunch between patients. She couldn't resist dusting his bookshelves and started pulling suits from his closet and taking them to the cleaners. She abandoned her own writing projects so she could spend her time editing a novel he had been trying to write for years. She even took over billing his dental patients.

In bed, she was primarily concerned with giving him pleasure—with doing the things he wanted her to do. Intercourse often started when he "playfully" pulled her pants down and spanked her. His spankings weren't brutal, but they did hurt, and hurting was clearly a part of his sexual excitement.

Ellen enjoyed being submissive, but she did wonder how far she was willing to go—and what might be required of her in a marriage with this man.

Ellen had come from a family that was difficult to please no matter how hard she tried. Her father was a petroleum consultant whom she remembered mostly from post cards of sand dunes and men dressed in white linen bathrobes. "Even when he was home," she said of him, "he had a way of still being in Afghanistan." Ellen's mother was devoted to the marriage. She spent her days pampering the furniture, running the children around in the family station wagon, and waiting for her husband to come home for a "visit." Ellen was not encouraged to help with the general house cleaning ("wait until you're a little older, Dear,") but was expected to keep her own room spotless. When her father was home, she watched her mother serve him dinner on the "for-company-only" tablecloth. If Ellen tried to clear the table afterward Mother would say, "That's all right, Dear. I'll do it." After dinner her father often dozed off in his chair, sometimes sleeping the whole night in the living room.

Ellen developed two important Psycho-Logic SETs ...

Ellen's "Sensitivity" Psycho-Logic

S. — Survival Assumption.

It's essential to have a relationship with someone who understands how I feel.

E. — Evaluation.

An ordinary man—like my father—is insensitive to my feelings.

T. — Tactic.

Marry a supersensitive man who seems truly interested in understanding me.

Ellen's "Slave Girl" Psycho-Logic

S. — Survival Assumption.

It's essential to get attention from the people I live with.

E. — Evaluation.

I got Mother's attention (and approval) by cleaning my room, and she got Dad's by waiting on him.

T. — Tactic.

Spend my life waiting on someone in order to get his attention.

When Ellen was ready to get married, she found herself a supersensitive dentist and started waiting on him.

Second Place Resentment

Ellen's dentist approached marriage from a different Psycho-Logic SET. He had come from a family of small-town physicians. His grandfather had started a general medical practice and his own father had carried it on. As an only son, Ellen's dentist fully intended to continue in the family tradition—until he failed his medical pre-entrance exams and was rejected by every school to which he applied. He reluctantly decided to take up dentistry as a "second choice."

Here is the Psycho-Logic that Ellen's dentist developed ...

"Second Best" Psycho-Logic

S. — Survival Assumption.

It's essential to be accepted.

E. — Evaluation.

The only way to be accepted in this family is to be a physician. I'm a failure because I'm not smart enough to be a physician.

T. — Tactic.

1. Second best is better than nothing (so go into dentistry).
2. Work hard and save all my money. Maybe that'll prove I'm okay.
3. I hate the people I love because they know I'm a failure. I take that hate out behind closed bedroom doors.

When Ellen first met her dentist he seemd to have the sensitivity she was looking for. She was willing to wait on him in exchange for his "understanding," but Ellen was not prepared for the degree of sexual submission required, or the underlying anger it implied. Her relationship ended four months after it began with Ellen accusing the dentist of "not really understanding her after all," and the dentist yelling at her that "pain is a natural part of sexual expression."

Super Pleaser

Frankie Geller was another client whose sexual Tactics emerged from his Psycho-Logic. Frankie was a rescuer—a self-proclaimed superman of the bed chambers, called to duty by desperate circumstance. By day he was a mild-mannered pharmaceutical assistant for a small metropolitan drug manufacturer. By night he disappeared into the secret chambers of a woman's bedroom, shed his work-a-day disguise and emerged as Super Pleaser, male rescuer of the sexually inadequate and downtrodden. "Look! Up in the bedroom! It's a *Playgirl* centerfold. It's a Masters-and-Johnson sexual surrogate! No, it's Frankie Geller!"

When he examined his sexual Psycho-Logic, it was easy for Frankie to see that rescuing was a large part of it. He had recently passed up a terrific date with a perfectly adequate woman in order to spend the night with a sexually frigid lady who had already left him disappointed several times—and this wasn't the first occasion when Frankie chose someone who "needed his help" over someone who had something to offer him.

Frankie's "Sexual Rescue" Psycho-Logic

S. — Survival Assumption.

It's important to be "needed" (loved and cared for).

E. — Evaluation.

People will *need* me if they *need me to help them* (sexualwise and otherwise).

T. — Tactic.

Find a mate who's inadequate so she will need me to help her with her inadequacy.

Sexual Regression

Next to opportunity, it's a person's Survival Assumptions, Evaluations, and Tactics that determine the quality of his or her sexual experience. Even in this age of women's emancipation, equal pay and equal opportunity do not always translate into equal bedroom behavior. Restrictive assumptions about what it means to be a man or a woman often make their last-ditch stand behind closed doors. Lingering inequality commonly revolves around the question of who runs things.

"Traditional Sex" Psycho-Logic

S. — Survival Assumption.

1. It's essential for a man to behave sexually in a "masculine" way, or
2. It's essential for a woman to behave like a woman (in order to feel "feminine").

E. — Evaluation.

When a man is "in charge," it makes him feel like a man and/or a woman feel like a woman. It turns both of them on.

T. — Tactics.

(as they are played out sexually).

1. The man initiates sex (or if the woman does, he's in charge of everything that follows).
2. The man is responsible for—
   a. Turning himself on (getting and keeping an erection).
   b. Turning her on (orchestrating a lengthy foreplay).
   c. Choosing entry timing and position and deciding when to roll over.
   d. Giving her at least one orgasm (and preferably several).
   e. Holding himself off until she is satisfied.
   f. Getting himself off.
   g. Cuddling and comforting her after they're finished.
3. The woman is responsible for—
   a. Birth control.
   b. Accepting his guidance.
   c. Fondling.
   d. Being cuddly and responsive.

The Change of Life

As we have seen, events can change Psycho-Logic—including traditional sexual Tactics. One client had always been proud of her "old-fashioned" sexual morality, until she suddenly found herself separated after thirteen years of marriage. When I first saw her, she was "fed up" with men—at least in any serious sense—although she was surprised to find that she was *not* fed up with sex. Her husband had been the only man she had actually slept with, although she "came close" once in high school. Her unexpected desire to see what other men were like was tinged with just enough guilt to enhance her anticipation. But when it happened the first time, she had such a hard time relaxing, her partner lost his interest. He left without saying goodbye. Sex wasn't turning out to be as much fun as she had hoped.

I asked her what she was trying to prove to herself.

"I guess that I could really go through with it," she said. "Or maybe to see if I could still attract someone."

We talked about how she wanted sex to fit into her life—what part she wanted it to play in a relationship. She finally decided that recreational sex was okay—at least in this point in her unmarried life—but that it would probably fit in a little better if she learned to relax with someone *before* she had sex with him.

Making Up for Lost Time

The ages and stages of life can sometimes create changes in sexual Psycho-Logic. There was something about being forty that made Edna take a hard look at her life—especially her sex life. Suddenly she couldn't be satisfied anymore. She started complaining that George was a "stick-in-the-mud." She wanted him to loosen up a little and enjoy himself more. Why didn't he buy her a vibrator for her birthday? George had never even seen a vibrator. Edna showed him one in her *Diverse Products Catalogue*. George had never seen a *Diverse Products Catalogue*.

Edna's sudden excitement was a little unsettling to George's sensible sexuality. All he could imagine was Edna hanging naked from the ceiling screaming because her vibrator batteries had burnt out. That was not George's idea of having fun. Maybe he *was* getting a little too old, or maybe Edna was getting a little too crazy.

Edna's "Now-or-Never" Psycho-Logic

S. — Survival Assumption.

It's essential to stay alive (need for physical survival).

E. — Evaluation.

Oh my God, I'm forty! Life is passing me by. I had better start living before it's too late.

T. — Tactics. (sexual)

1. Disregard my "childish" inhibitions.
2. Get George to liven up a bit.

When Edna finally explained to George how she felt about growing old, it was a little easier for him to sympathize—he felt less threatened, and he did loosen up some. He even placed an order with Diverse Products. Edna never did hang from the ceiling, but she did start hanging onto George a little tighter and a little longer.

Mutual Satisfaction

Just as it takes two people to develop satisfying sexual Tactics it takes two people to iron out Tactical differences. When each one of them understands the other's Psycho-Logic, there's a much better chance of developing Counter Logic solutions that meet both their needs.

Mary Ann turned a cold back when Jody rubbed his hand down her thigh. He sighed his disappointment.

"What do you expect?" she asked him. "I can't argue with you all day and turn on when the lights go out!"

Mary Ann's "Love-Sex" Psycho-Logic

S. — Survival Assumption.

Love is *the essential element* of a marriage or a caring relationship.

E. — Evaluation.

Sex is an expression of my love for Jody.

T. — Tactic.

I can't feel sexy while I'm feeling hostile and angry.

Jody's "Light-Switch Sex" Psycho-Logic

S. — Survival Assumption.

Sex is an important part in a loving relationship.

E. — Evaluation.

Mary Ann—the woman I love—is sexually exciting and stimulating.

T. — Tactic.

When I see her naked or feel her next to me, I try something.

Mary Ann sometimes felt that Jody was insensitive. ("If he really loved me he wouldn't try anything when I wasn't feeling like it.") Jody felt the same about her. ("If she cared about me, she'd be more concerned with *my* needs.")

I told them I thought they both had a point. But instead of giving out "Ms. or Mr. Right" awards, maybe we could use our time to figure out how to make things work better. We figured out the Psycho-Logic each was operating from and wrote it out on a chalkboard. Then I asked them to take a look at it as if it were another couple they didn't know. Did they see any things this couple could do to please each other without compromising too much on what they wanted for themselves?

This is the Counter Logic they came up with...

"Sexual Thoughtfulness" Counter Logic

Counter Logic	Sex doesn't work for us unless both of us feel like having it.
Jody's Counter Tactics	1. Don't approach Mary Ann for sex unless I've been treating her nicely for at least an hour before I try. (Turn her on by being sincerely nice to her first.) 2. Find little ways to show her I love her and that I'm not just out to use her (like helping her with the dishes, thoughtfulness, and nonsexual hugs). 3. Talk to her more about *her* sexual feelings instead of just telling her what I like.
Mary Ann's Counter Tactics	1. When I *am* feeling sexy, approach Jody for a change. 2. Put more thought into sex. If sex is an expression of my love for Jody, love him in a way that he really appreciates. 3. When I'm *not* feeling turned on, find ways to turn him down gently—and lovingly.

They decided to try out their Tactics. In two weeks both were pleased with their progress. Each could see that the other was genuinely trying. That was at least as important as anything they were doing.

Sensate Focus

Working out sexual differences often amounts to a search for a common ground—a mutually acceptable Counter Logic approach, but sometimes a sexual problem is more in the individual than in the relationship. A person who is excessively shy or anxious may have problems having sex with even the most agreeable and willing partner. In this case, the person may need to develop an individual Counter Logic approach to handle his shyness or anxiety.

Masters and Johnson have developed a Counter Logic approach that has helped overcome a number of sexual difficulties and inhibitions. They called their technique *Sensate Focus*. It requires the individual to concentrate on his *sensuality* rather than his *sexuality*. By focusing on pure sensory experience, his anxiety is automatically reduced and his sexual satisfaction—the quality of his experience—is greatly enhanced.

When you think about it, sexual intercourse is the most pure concentration of *sensual* experience a person can have. It arouses and delights all five of the senses—taste, smell, sight, hearing, and touch.

Tom Jones Eats Again

Children are much more attuned to their senses than adults. As we grow older, our senses get dulled through their physical deterioration. Our grown-up senses also get dulled in the rush of life. Nothing seems to stand out among the mass of stimuli that constantly whirl around us, but it is possible to touch the earth again and feel its coolness and its dampness—to notice things we were once more aware of. We can reopen our ears and hear the birds and crickets singing in the night. And we can re-experience the natural beauty of the human body and celebrate its warmth and wetness and softness. It is only through the experience of being fully alive in the physical world that we can truly approach the fullness of our sexuality.

Anyone who has seen the movie "Tom Jones" knows what a sensual and *sexual* experience eating a meal can be...

Tom's whore runs her tongue across the furry, velvet skin of
a firm ripe peach, lightly biting into the skin and slowly sucking

it's juice into her mouth. Moving her lips gently across the edge of the outer skin and over the silky moist inner meat, the warm liquid dripping down her chin and the sweet smell of the open fruit filling Tom's nostrils. The fruit savored in her mouth, tossed gently back and forth, and then slowly swallowed while looking directly into the eyes of her lover.

No verbal message need be added to this message of physical delight and pure sensual pleasure. Tom Jones knew how to ride a horse in the wind, run naked in the summer rain, feel the touch of cool mountain water, and romp in the hay with his lover. Sensuality was not something he turned on for sex and turned off for everything else. It was simply a way of relating to life.

The Flowering of Mr. Gurney

Mr. Gurney came for counseling because he couldn't get an erection with his wife. He wanted to please her—if only to get her off his back—but his body just wouldn't cooperate.

Mr. Gurney had lost interest in all sorts of pleasures. He spent most of his evenings in front of his TV—seldom bothering to change the channel. By 7:30 he would have to think to tell you what he had for dinner an hour earlier. He used to cultivate a garden in the summer but he gave that up a couple of years earlier—too much work. He did take some interest in his job, but that was about all.

Mr. Gurney needed help with more than just his sexual problem, but as his therapy progressed he did hit upon an effective sexual Counter Logic that he found quite useful. The idea came from a dream he told me about, which he said was "definitely sexual"— although it wasn't about sex. It was about flowers. I asked him to describe exactly what he *saw* in his dream.

"I was in a flower store—looking for something. I didn't know what at first. Then I remembered I was supposed to go to a dance—as if I were back in high school again. I needed a corsage for my date. She wasn't in the dream though. The man in the flower store was telling me that the prettiest flowers were the most delicate. They had to be sprayed all the time to keep them damp. The man opened the door to the flower case, but the cold air fogged up my glasses and I didn't see anything at first. Then the man reached out and wiped one of my lenses with his handkerchief and for a few seconds I could see he was holding an orchid—the most beautiful orchid I ever saw. It seemed overwhelming. I couldn't say anything. I was crying in the dream. Then I woke up. I remember noticing I had an erection. It felt good. I just lay there for awhile—kind of in an afterglow."

After he described his dream, I told him I wanted him to consider the very natural relationship between those warm, sexual, dream feelings, and the act of having sex with his wife, but first I wanted him to try relating them in his imagination. I asked him to lean back in his chair, close his eyes and concentrate for a moment on letting the tension flow from his body, until he felt comfortably relaxed. When he seemed at ease, I asked him to reconstruct his dream image of that beautifully sensual orchid. I told him he could now see it quite vividly, with only a faint mist surrounding it. When I saw him nod his head, I told him to pay particular attention to the lacy silk texture of his imagined orchid, and then to focus on the violet-pink colors as they shaded off into the darkness of valleys and ridges, and then take a few seconds to notice the soft moisture as some of it beaded up and gently rolled down one of the flower petals, while the rest of the moisture covered the petals like a soft misty protection. Now I wanted him to hold this image, but to recapture those spontaneous sexual feelings he experienced in the afterglow of his dream—and to see their source in the beautiful sensuality of the flower. If he got an erection while he was lying there thinking about it, that was fine. If he didn't, that was fine, too.

Now I wanted him to bring even more of his *creative* imagination into play. Ever so slowly, while still holding the picture and the feeling of this beautiful orchid in his mind, I wanted him gradually to become aware of the striking similarity between the shapes and folds of the orchid petals, and the shapes and folds of his wife's vagina. I wanted him to notice similarity between the wetness and the soft, violet-pink colors. After he had captured this, I wanted him to actually see his mental picture of the orchid and his wife's vagina begin to merge in his imagination—dissolving slowly from one and then slowly back again into the other. If he began to lose the erotic feelings that went with the orchid, I wanted him to bring the orchid back into focus again and, at the same time, allow his erotic feelings to return as the flower came back. Then I wanted him to slowly dissolve the orchid back to the vagina again, holding onto his sexual feelings during the transformation. Flower to vagina, back and forth—until feelings and images seemed to melt together in his imagination.

After focusing on this moving image for several sessions, spread out over an hour, he said he was maintaining a good erection through most of it. He was ready to put his erection to a test. I told him to proceed slowly—and to tell his wife what he was doing, so she could help him get used to her renewed erotic pleasures. When her legs were open, and he was looking at her vagina, I wanted him to lovingly survey the similarity between what he saw in front of him, and his orchid dream image. I wanted him to fully appreciate the secret beauty that was now revealed to him. If he had to, he could close his eyes for several seconds to refocus on his orchid image and to re-energize his sexual feelings. When he had gotten a full, hard erection, and a sexual feeling to sustain it, I wanted him to have intercourse with his wife but I wanted him to close his eyes and imagine slipping his penis between the stiffened, wet petals of the orchid. When he was almost at climax, I wanted him to dissolve that mental orchid into a sharp, clear image of his wife's wet, pulsating vagina, and ejaculate inside it.

Mr. Gurney was eventually able to get an erection by turning himself on with his own image. He found a personalized Counter Logic that focused his attention on his own erotic sensuality. It was hardly the end of his therapy, but he knew he was moving in the right direction.

Sexual Counter Logic

You don't have to have a sexual problem to create a more satisfying sexual experience. By focusing on specific Counter Logic you may be able to devise Tactics that add significantly to the quality of your sexual relationships.

Sensate yourself. When you participate in the sensual delights of the world, sex becomes a theme in the midst of a symphony...

- Take off your clothes and stand up straight and tall in front of a full-length mirror.
- Walk on the beach in the early morning and feel the sand pushing up between your toes.
- Run the smooth pages of a new book across your cheeks and smell the printer's ink.

- Turn off all the lights and noises, and listen to your favorite music in the stillness of yourself.
- Stretch out on a thick rug in front of the fireplace on a snowy winter's evening.
- Close your eyes on a foggy night and listen to a train whistle, or a ship crying in the darkness.
- Rub the tummy of an animal and really feel the warmth and velvet softness of its fur.
- Smell a woman's hair after it's freshly shampooed.
- Watch the birth of a rose as it slowly unfolds its petals and exposes its color and its aroma.
- Hold the taste of a lobster in your mouth a few seconds before swallowing it.
- Stand with your back to the ocean waves and feel the weight of them wrap around you, and the foam bubble up over your shoulders and around your neck.
- Cuddle in the nude with the person you love. Sense the coolness, the smoothness, the aroma, and the taste of the other's body.

Use it or lose it. Sexual desire ebbs and flows, but within this changing rhythm, the more sex you have the more desire you generate. The more you ignore your desire, the more it withers away.

Have a love affair with your body. You don't have to be perfect to appreciate your own inherent beauty. The human body, in and of itself, is naturally beautiful—a miracle of organic chemistry, reproductive biology, spontaneous growth, and rhythmic mechanical function. The more you appreciate what you have, the more you appreciate the joy that comes from it.

Make love in love. Making love is more fun, and more meaningful, when you do it with someone you genuinely care for. When you love the person you are making love to, you give that person more than your body—you give yourself.

"After talk." Trial and error can teach you the obvious things another person likes, but guessing and nonverbal communication can only take you so far. Some things just can't be communicated by grunts and moans—they have to be said in words. When you spend

time sharing your sexual desires and fantasies you discover much more about each other than your sexual preferences.

Enjoy playful spontaneity. Variety is the spice of life—especially the sexual life. Like a good dinner, good sex is often a result of "planned spontaneity"—a combination or forethought and responding to the delights of the moment. The same dinner every night gets just as boring as the same kind of sex. So spice things up occasionally.

Sex as a relationship gauge. When sex isn't working well, there's a good chance that something in the relationship isn't working. Most sexual problems are *relationship* problems—sometimes temporary, sometimes serious. In either case, they represent an opportunity to talk things over with your partner—to see what each of you wants from sex, and how each of you is using it. It's an opportunity to better understand each other's sexual Psycho-Logic. The better your Psycho-Logic works, the better your anatomy functions.

References

Page

Chapter 3

44   Terkel, Studs. Roberta Victor, hooker. *Working.* New York: Pantheon Books, Random House, 1972.

Chapter 6

87   Sulton-Smith, Brian and Rosenberg, B.G. *The Sibling.* New York: Holt, Rinehart and Winston, 1970.

Chapter 7

98   Sheehy, Gail. *Passages.* New York: Dutton, 1976.

Chapter 8

114   Smith, Adam. *Powers of Mind.* New York: Random House, 1975.

115   Gallwey, Timothy. *Inner Tennis: Playing the Game.* New York: Random House, 1976.

116   Schulman, Michael. "Backstage Behaviorism." *Psychology Today,* June, 1973, pg. 51.

116   Reyher, J. & Smeltzer, W. "The Uncovering Properties of Visual Imagery and Verbal Association: A Comparative Study." *Journal of Abnormal Psychology.* 1968, 73, 218-222.

117   Crampton, M. "The Use of Mental Imagery in Psychosynthesis." *Journal of Humanistic Psychology,* 1969, 9, 139-153.

Chapter 9

125   Roosevelt, Sara Delano. As told to Leighton, Isabelle and Forbush, Gabrielle. *My Boy Franklin.* New York: R. Long & P. R. Smith, 1933.

Chapter 10

134   Lerner, Alan J. *Camelot*. New York: Random House, 1961.
139   Therapy of Depression. *60 Minutes*. Produced by CBS Television News, November, 1976.
145   Wexler, David A. "Self-Actualization and Cognitive Processes." *Journal of Consulting and Clinical Psychology*, 1974, 47-53.

Chapter 11

150   Suinn, Richard. "Body Thinking: Psychology for Olympic Champs." *Psychology Today*, July, 1966, pg. 35.
150   Gallwey, Timothy. *Inner Tennis: Playing the Game*. New York: Random House, 1976.
152   Horan, John (et al.), *Journal of Consulting and Clinical Psychology*, 43, 1.
153   Lazarus, Arnold. "Behavior Therapy and Beyond." In *Behavior Research and Therapy*. New York: McGraw-Hill, 1971.

Chapter 12

160   Dyer, Wayne W. *Your Erroneous Zones*. New York: Funk & Wagnalls, 1976, pg. 63.

Chapter 13

175   Ullmann, Liv. *Changing*. New York: Knopf, 1977.
176   Siegel, Alberta. "Only Twenty Years Left." Speech to the new members of Phi Beta Kappa, Stanford University, as reported in *The Stanford Observer*, 1973.

Chapter 15

202   Frankl, Viktor. *Man's Search for Meaning*. Boston: Beacon Press, 1959.

Chapter 16

212   Albee, Edward. *Who's Afraid of Virginia Woolf?* A play. New York: Atheneum, 1962.

Chapter 17

229   Masters, William H. and Johnson, Virginia. *The Pleasure Bond*. Boston: Little, Brown, 1975.

Index